William Wagner

From Classroom Dummy to University President

World of Theology Series

Published by the Theological Commission of the World Evangelical Alliance

Volume 16

Vol 1	Thomas K. Johnson: The First Step in Missions Training: How our Neighbors are Wrestling with God's General Revelation
Vol 2	Thomas K. Johnson: Christian Ethics in Secular Cultures
Vol 3	David Parker: Discerning the Obedience of Faith: A Short History of the World Evangelical Alliance Theological Commission
Vol 4	Thomas Schirrmacher (Ed.): William Carey: Theologian – Linguist – Social Reformer
Vol 5	Thomas Schirrmacher: Advocate of Love – Martin Bucer as Theologian and Pastor
Vol 6	Thomas Schirrmacher: Culture of Shame / Culture of Guilt
Vol 7	Thomas Schirrmacher: The Koran and the Bible
Vol 8	Thomas Schirrmacher (Ed.): The Humanisation of Slavery in the Old Testament
Vol 9	Jim Harries: New Foundations for Appreciating Africa: Beyond Religious and Secular Deceptions
Vol 10	Thomas Schirrmacher: Missio Dei – God's Missional Nature
Vol 11	Thomas Schirrmacher: Biblical Foundations for 21st Century World Mission
Vol 12	William Wagner, Mark Wagner: Can Evangelicals Truly Change the World? How Seven Philosophical and Religious Movements Are Growing
Vol 13	Thomas Schirrmacher: Modern Fathers
Vol 14	Jim Harries: Jarida juu ya Maisha ya MwAfrika katika huduma ya Ukristo
Vol 15	Peter Lawrence: Fellow Travellers – A Comparative Study on the Identity Formation of Jesus Followers from Jewish, Christian and Muslim Backgrounds in The Holy Land
Vol 16	William Wagner: From Classroom Dummy to University President – Serving God in the Land of Sound of Music

William Wagner

From Classroom Dummy to University President

Serving God in the Land of Sound of Music

WIPF & STOCK · Eugene, Oregon

Wipf and Stock Publishers
199 W 8th Ave, Suite 3
Eugene, OR 97401

From Classroom Dummy to University President
Serving God in the Land of Sound of Music
By Wagner, William
Copyright © 2020 Verlag für Kultur und Wissenschaft
Culture and Science Publ. All rights reserved.
Softcover ISBN-13: 978-1-7252-8970-3
Publication date 10/23/2020
Previously published by Verlag für Kultur und Wissenschaft
Culture and Science Publ., 2020

Contents

Foreword (by Dr. Heinrich Derksen) 7
Foreword (by Colonel Charles Reynolds) 9
Preface 11
Acknowledgements 12
Dedication 13

Chapter 1: Family Roots 15
Chapter 2: Failure in School 21
Chapter 3: Facts on Dyslexia 27
Chapter 4: Formation and Development 33
Chapter 5: Football Success 39
Chapter 6: Faith in Christ 45
Chapter 7: Father's Inspiration 53
Chapter 8: Faithful "Mitarbeiters" 65
Chapter 9: Foreign Missions 73
Chapter 10: Freedom in the Spirit 89
Chapter 11: Further Studies 97
Chapter 12: Finding New Directions 105
Chapter 13: Faculty Status 119
Chapter 14: Future Possibilities 131

Foreword

By Dr. Heinrich Derksen

You are holding in your hands a book that is more than simply an autobiography. This book reveals the greatness of God in the life of a man. It describes how God changes lives, and how he uses people who make themselves available to him.

I have always admired the dedication of Bill and Sally Wagner, who served as missionaries in Europe for so many years. Bill's vision and talent for networking have inspired and drawn many people together throughout his lifetime. His love of learning and example as a life-long learner have motived many. His faith in God and belief in accomplishing the impossible have deeply impacted me and have changed the trajectory of both my life and that of Bible Seminary Bonn.

I met Bill Wagner for the first time in 1995. As a young professor at Bible Seminary Bonn, I sat in on his lecture as he taught the discipleship course, "Master Life." His passion and deep conviction as a teacher and his love for Jesus and toward lost people both inspired and motivated me. Bill has always been a forward-thinker and was often one step ahead when it came to trying a new path or testing new concepts. Since he began teaching at Bible Seminary Bonn in the early 1990's, he has helped to shape the development of the school and has left his mark on hundreds of students.

Bill was also instrumental in helping Bible Seminary Bonn to develop theological partnerships in the USA. First in a partnership with Golden Gate Baptist Theological Seminary, and then in transferring to a partnership with Southwestern Baptist Theological Seminary, he was the bridge-builder between the two institutions.

We held our first discussions about a partnership with Southwestern Baptist Theological Seminary with Dr. Ken Hemphill, who was the president at the time. But then Dr. Paige Patterson became the president of SWBTS in October 2003. We definitely wanted to move forward with the partnership, and I requested that our board permit me to fly to the USA. Because we were in a financial crisis at that time, the board told me that it was a waste of money to fly there. So, Willi Daiker and I planned to travel to the USA, covering the costs ourselves, and meet Bill Wagner in November 2003, even though we did not yet have a meeting scheduled with the new president. Bill Wagner remained confident that we would get an appointment with Dr. Patterson.

Just before leaving Germany, we did receive notice of an appointment available for a brief meeting on the day that we landed in the USA. So, we planned to meet Bill Wagner at the car rental location at DFW in Dallas and travel together to the appointment with Dr. Patterson, but our flight got delayed. Bill sat in the car outside the airport, waiting and praying. After some time, it became apparent that if we didn't arrive soon, we would miss the meeting. He said to God: "I'll wait until the next bus arrives from the airport, and then I'm leaving!" He would have had to meet with Dr. Patterson alone on our behalf, but God answered our prayers and his, and we were on the next bus.

It was downpouring, and we left the airport much later than planned. It was rush hour, and the highway was packed. But Bill searched for ways to slip through traffic. We finally arrived exhausted but on time to our meeting with the president. He warmly received us, and a short time later he started a partnership with Bible Seminary Bonn. This experience deeply changed me, my life, and that of our seminary.

I am grateful to this day to Bill Wagner for his readiness to help and to use his connections to build-up the kingdom of God. He goes down paths and opens doors that others don't even see. He has often seen the impossible and with God's help achieved it.

When my family and I vacationed in the USA a few years ago, Bill and Sally welcomed us to their home and showered us with warm hospitality. Hanging on the wall in their home, there was a woodcarving inscribed with Bill's motto: "For to me to live is Christ!" In this sense, Bill Wagner is a hero of the faith for me, and this book is a wonderful testimony of his life-long pursuit of that goal.

I thank Bill that through this book, he gives God all the glory, and is an example to many! May this book bring you joy as you read!

Dr. Heinrich Derksen
Dean, Bible Seminary Bonn

Foreword

By Colonel Charles Reynolds

The greatest legacy we leave on this earth is the investment of our time in shaping the lives of others. I only worked with Bill Wagner for one year, but that year was one of the most formative in my development as a minister.

Of the many attributes I admired in Bill, the most important was his close relationship with God, exemplified in his prayer life. The first week we met, Bill and I, along with Journeyman Drexel Rayford, drove from Innsbruck Austria to Brussels Belgium, where Bill was scheduled to preach a revival at the International Baptist Church. We had planned to spend the night in Frankfurt. We had not anticipated having any difficulty in finding a hotel room in one of Germany's largest cities, but on that particular weekend there was an international automobile race being held near the city. We had attempted to find a room in several hotels. All were full and unable to refer us to any other hotel with a vacancy. After returning to the car after yet another unsuccessful enquiry, Bill bowed his head and prayed this simple prayer. "OK, Lord, you have sent us on this trip to serve you, and we are counting on you to provide us a place to sleep." The next hotel we tried had just opened and had not been booked for the auto show. In addition, as a promotion, a free meal was provided with booking a room. After unloading our suitcases, we met in the dining room. We expressed our gratitude to God and I feasted on my first German Pfeffer Steak. I soon learned prayers such as these were common when working with Bill. Whenever we faced a challenge that year, Bill would simply bow his head and say, "OK, Lord," and give the problem to God.

Bill never micromanaged. I remember well the first assignment he gave me. "Charlie, find out where there are American students in Innsbruck, and start a Bible study." That was all he said, but the tone of his voice conveyed his faith in my ability, and inspired a sense of confidence that I would accomplish the task. The only American students in Innsbruck were from Notre Dame University. They were all raised Roman Catholic, but in a few months, 26 of the 42 students were on a Bible study retreat, learning how to pray Bill Wagner-style prayers, from a Southern Baptist Journeyman. A year later, circumstances required Bill and his family to return to the US, leaving a 22-year-old journeyman in charge of the Innsbruck mission. Bill took me out for dinner the night before he was to leave. I sat across the table awaiting his parting words of wisdom. "Well Charlie," Bill said with a smile on his face, as I waited in anticipation, "sink or swim." Not exactly the words I had anticipated; however, Bill's tone let me know that he was confident that I would keep my head above water. Bill's example had given me tools that I needed to do so, not only for that year, but for the rest of my ministry.

Another important attribute I acquired from Bill, was the importance of viewing other ministers as colleagues, not rivals. One would expect that Christian missionaries, even though they were from different faith groups, would get along and work together. Unfortunately, this was rarely the reality. For Bill, if you were a Christian missionary, you were on the same team. We had missionaries from three different mission organizations working in our church. I remember, Bill taking some heat for allowing a missionary who was not Southern Baptist use our mission van to take some church members from another church, on a mission trip. For Bill all that mattered was that they were doing ministry. Bill's example prepared me to serve as a military chaplain, where I would need to be comfortable working with chaplains from many faith groups.

If I had to limit my description of Bill to two words, those words would be contagious energy. Everything Bill did, he did with gusto; and he challenged others to do the same. Bill was always pushing you to achieve your best for God. Bill would often ask me, "when are you going to be the Chief of Chaplains." I did not quite meet that expectation, but in part to Bill's encouragement, I was a successful Chaplain reaching the rank of Colonel, directed the Army Center for World Religions, and served as the Command Chaplain for US Army Africa and as the Strategic Religious Advisor for US Forces in Iraq.

The best part of knowing Bill Wagner was knowing his family. Five thousand miles away from my own, Bill, Sally, Candace and Mark became my family that year. My prayer as you read "From Classroom Dummy to University President," is that Bill's life will impact your life and ministry as much as it has mine.

Colonel Charles (Charlie) Reynolds
Missionary Journeyman in Innsbruck Austria 1977-79

Preface

One of the most famous early Christian Fathers was Polycarp, the Bishop of Smyrna, one of the seven churches of Asia. We still have many of his writings on the faith. In the Roman Empire in approximately 155 B.C., there was another push to recognize that the Roman Caesar should be worshiped as a God. In Smyrna, the political leaders decreed that all must burn incense to Cesar as a means of recognizing his deity. Polycarp refused and was thus brought before the authorities and told of the potential consequences of his decision to not burn the incense. Polycarp has been quoted as saying, "Eighty and six years I have served Him, and He has done me no wrong. How can I blaspheme my King and Savior? Bring forth what thou wilt." Soon thereafter he was burned at the stake.

I originally read this quote from the *Halley Bible Handbook,* one of my first books on theology. My prayer at that time was that my God would also allow me to also serve Him for eighty-six years. At this time, I have been ordained as a Southern Baptist pastor for over sixty-two years, and I hope that my time of service will continue.

My reason for writing this book is quite simple. It is not to show what I have done but to allow others to see how God can and does work in the lives of men and women today regardless of their circumstances. My life is not different from others, but I must admit that He has allowed me to have many special experiences that I want to share. As I wrote this book, I was keenly aware that so much of the book about me, but I had a hard time trying to write an autobiographical book without talking too much about myself. So much of who I am is because of how much other people poured their lives into mine. I have tried to name the many with whom I have had the privilege to work. Some are named, but it is not possible to list all those who have been a real influence in my life, so I fear that I have left many out. Still the Lord's blessings have been so many that I felt compelled to write down all He has done for me and through me. This book is not about one missionary, but about the wonderful grace of our God who blesses those who desire to serve Him. God still calls his people to put on the mantle left by others who have done missionary work for the sake of the Kingdom. Today He still calls many to give up everything to serve him. God is not yet done with us. He continues to use us.

Once while living in Europe I was listening to a BBC announcer talking about the remarks made by one British politician about another politician. The first politician stated, "He is not an extraordinary man, but he has made extraordinary use of the man he is." I was deeply touched by these words, and at that time I decided to make extraordinary use of the man I am.

Acknowledgements

In this book it is very apparent that both my core family as well as my extended family have done much in shaping who I am. The book is mainly about how God takes one of his creations and molds him to fit into his plan, but an important part of the works of God is that He uses other people to help us become what God desires that we be. My family is extremely important, as the pages of this book will adequately relate. As I look out into today's world, I see many trying to make it in life, but lack a supporting family. Once again, I thank my God for Sally, my wife, Candice, my daughter, and Mark, my son. All three have been and are today steady warriors for Jesus as were those family members who have gone before me, even going back four and five generations. That is why this book starts with the family.

As I relook at my life, I remember several who taught me and helped me, starting with my first pastor, Rev. Stanley Unruh. He was nothing but a small church pastor, but for me he was a mighty, steady rock who helped lay the spiritual foundation for many years of service. One significant seminary professor was Dr. J. D. Hughey, who later became the Area Director for Europe from the Foreign Mission Board of the Sothern Baptists. Another theology professor who impressed me with both his knowledge and ability to practically apply his knowledge was Dr. Rick Durst from Golden Gate Baptist Theological Seminary. I owe him a great debt of gratitude.

A later inspiration was Dr. David Jang. My many years of working with him have shown him to be a solid evangelical theologian and one of the more creative thinkers I have ever worked with. He formed the Olivet University and continues to do the impossible for the Lord.

Also, not to be forgotten is Dr. Thomas Schirrmacher, a truly inspirational world class German leader who has served the World Evangelical Alliance well. His vision to create a publishing house for Christian literature both encouraged me and helped in getting this and other books out into the wider public.

Dedication

This book is dedicated to my lovely wife Sally. For over sixty-four years she has stood with me through both the mountain peaks of life as well the deep valleys and the disappointments of life. She would never complain but would hold my arms up high when the going was difficult.

Now she is suffering from an extended illness that has made it necessary for me to be by her side and to encourage her and to help her. Without her love and encouragement, it would have been impossible for us to serve our Lord in the way we did.

I dedicate this book to her.

Sally Wagner as a Model

Chapter 1

Family Roots

> "The happiest moments of my life have been
> the few which I have passed at home in
> the bosom of my family."
> – Thomas Jefferson

Echoes of the Plains

In my church I have just finished a series of sermons on Abraham, Isaac, and Jacob. If one follows the golden thread of God working in the life of these three men, it is easy to see the importance of one generation's influence upon the following generations. From a negative point of view, the Bible says that the sins of a man affect the lives of those in the family for five generations. Although we often fail to see it, the same can be said of the good works that a family does. Blessings will be felt by those in the following generations. Just as the godly behavior of Abraham, Isaac, and Jacob led to blessings for many generations, so I have been blessed by those of my family who came before me.

I am lucky to have a history of great pioneers in my family. One was a great, great aunt, Ellen Crockford Canaga, who wrote a book about her family's experiences in the second half of the nineteenth century. Her family left the good life in Michigan and traveled by covered wagon to Nebraska and then on to South Dakota. In her book she tells many stories of both the hardships of life on the plains and the mercies of God in what was then an underdeveloped area of the country. They lived through famines, floods, animal attacks, and illness.

One of her stories is about a time in Nebraska when the family was going to church in their horse drawn wagon. They were attacked by an angry bison. Her husband jumped out of the wagon to protect the family and took the animal on with his bare hands. According to the book, the man was lifted between the horns of the bison, and after riding around in that position for a while, he took out his knife and slit the throat of the bruising animal. He saved the family. In another story her brother was attacked by a grizzly bear, and he also had only a knife with which to defend himself. After a long fight he killed the bear, but he died the next day from his injuries.

Once when they were homesteading in South Dakota, the soldiers from the nearby fort came by and warned them that a group of warring Indians were coming their way. The soldiers told the family that they needed to pack up and move to the fort for protection. They stopped by their neighbor's house and gave them the warning. As they spoke with the neighbors, the father of that family said that they had had other warnings previously and nothing ever came of them, so they were going to stay home. My ancestral family went to the fort and stayed for about a week before they were told they could go home since the Indians had passed. On their way home, they went by their neighbor's house where they found that it had been burned to the ground, and the whole family had been killed and scalped. Life was not easy on the frontier.

Some historians like to divide peoples of that time into two groups. One group was the settlers, those who were satisfied with where they lived, while the second group was the pioneers, or those who were always ready to accept new challenges and move if necessary. My family on both sides were the pioneers, possessing a trait that I seem to have inherited. It is the pioneers who never ask why; instead, they always ask why not.

Opal and Pearl helping their Father

Sturgis, South Dakota:

Today if one mentions the town of Sturgis, most will recognize it as the Motorcycle Capital of the country where once a year the largest number of motorcyclists in the U.S.A. gather for a gigantic meeting. In 2015 they set a record and drew more than one million visitors. Sturgis, however, it is also the place where my mother was born and grew up. The small house where she spent her childhood still stands on the outskirts of Sturgis. Mother, whose first name was Opal, had an identical twin sister by the name of Pearl. Her father, who died while the girls were still small, was a traveling salesman for Wards products, and he often used the two beautiful twin girls as a drawing card to sell his products. After her husband's death my grandmother became a cook and eventually moved to work at the South Dakota Schools of Mines cafeteria in Rapid City, South Dakota. Neither of the two girls had much education, quitting school after the eighth grade.

A Fatherless Father

Dad's extended family also eventually reach South Dakota, where one of my great, great uncles bought a hotel in the town of Deadwood, which is also known for certain historical events. According to a recent book, Buffalo Bill Cody spent a night in the Wagner Hotel; the next day he was killed at a poker game in the bar adjacent to the hotel.

Lead, South Dakota, was my dad's hometown. When he was just nine months old his father left his mother and the two children because he said that he did not want the responsibility of supporting a family. His father's departure left the family destitute. His mother took in laundry, and my dad began to work at the age of six to help pay the bills. Among the jobs he did as a ten-year-old child were delivering mail and working as a miner in the local Homestake gold mine. Although he worked hard, he still managed to finish high school. He was able to play football, and he received a football scholarship to the South Dakota School of Mines that paid his tuition but not his board and room. He was extremely poor, so the president of the school gave him and his close friend permission to sleep in the furnace room that was in the basement of a college building. Having a place to sleep was a help, but he still lacked funds for food. Eventually, the cook at the school's cafeteria saw their plight and told them that if they came to the back door after all the others had eaten, she would give them the leftovers. Thus, every evening the two boys would wait for their daily food. The cook would give the food to her twin daughters who would then deliver it to the two hungry students. One of those twins was my mother.

Dad always was a free-spirited person, and even during his time in the university he took off a year and became what was for the time the equivalent of a hippy. He became a real hobo, sneaking on freight trains and going cross country, living off gifts of free food and enjoying the life of a vagabond. He did, however, decide to go back to school after a year of adventure.

While Dad was a student, a group of men came to the South Dakota School of Mines in Rapid City where Dad was studying and wanted some students to take their party up one of the mountains close to the school. The mountain in question was also near where Dad had grown up, and he knew it well; thus, he and another student volunteered to lead the party. They spent the night on the top of the mountain, and the next day the men studied it. The mountain was named Rushmore, and the leader of the men was the famous sculptor Gutzon Borglum. In the museum at Mount Rushmore, there is a photo of the first campfire on the mountain; my dad was a part of this group.

Despite the hardships, Dad finished his degree in civil engineering at the South Dakota School of Mines. By this time, he and my mother were married. He enjoyed the study in civil engineering and decided to go on for a master's degree at Iowa State. After finishing his studies, he found work in Los Angeles. Their family's life was good until the depression hit and he lost his job. To provide for his family, he worked as a ditch digger for two years before God seemed to smile upon him and he was offered a job as a Professor of Engineering at the rather isolated University of New Mexico. At that time New Mexico had only been a state for twenty years and it still had the flavor or an early wild west town. He gladly accepted the position and later became the Chairman of The Civil Engineering Department. Mother always felt like a misfit since she was a faculty wife but had never attended even high school. This lack was always a problem for her since most of the other wives had university degrees, but she never ceased to be the simple country woman she had always been.

Because Dad had inherited a pioneering spirit, he accomplished much in his position. He received credit for creating the New Mexico Branch of the National Society of Professional Engineers (NSPE) and held the number one engineering license for the state. He also was elected to be the vice president of the National NSPE. Early in the 1950s there was no formal testing of building materials in the state. Dad recognized a need for testing; thus, in his spare time be founded the Albuquerque Testing Laboratory, which did material testing for builders and for the government.

This laboratory was one of the earliest in the country and later became one of the largest in the Southwest. This enterprise eventually grew to the point that it had thirty employees.

Dad never forgot his father. He knew he was still alive and often tried to locate him, but every attempt ended in failure. Finally, about 1957 the news came that my grandpa was in Denver, selling Christmas trees. Dad went to Denver and contacted his father, a homeless, defeated man who lived in a tin and cardboard lean-to close to Golden. Grandpa accepted my dad's invitation to move to Albuquerque and live with my family. I was able to get to know him as we shared our home with him until he died.

Bill and Opal Wagner being honored by his students

Inherited Advantages:

During my early years, my father was not a Christian although he did accept Christ later in life at a revival where I was preaching. My mother had a deep faith and thus always sent me to Sunday School although she seldom went herself until I was in junior high school. I consider her desire for me to carry on the legacy of a true faith in God as a family benefit. Also, in looking at the history of my family, it becomes apparent that only those who had good health survived the hardships of being pioneers, and I feel that my good health is because of an inherited DNA that goes with being from a pioneer family. I also inherited a simple form of life that went with those who lived on the plains. God seems to have taken the history of my family and used it to help mold me into the person I am.

CHAPTER 2

Failure in School

> "If I could get the ear of every young man but for one word, it would be this: make the most and best of yourself. There is no tragedy like a wasted life-a life failing of its true end, and turned to a false end."
> – T.T. Munger

My Parents' Philosophy of Child Raising

During my parents' growing up years, South Dakota was a beautiful state with few people to fill its spaces; thus, both my parents were given the opportunity to run around in the open as young children. As my parents had children, they retained this attitude. I imagine that today both my parents would be arrested for child abuse. They gave us a great amount of freedom of movement.

One counselor once told me that an important aspect of raising children has to do with love and freedom. He made a grid with the horizontal line being love or no love while the vertical line was strict or freedom. This is the grid he used.

	Love	No Love
Strict	Strict with Love	Strict with no Love
Freedom	Freedom with Love	Freedom with no Love

My upbringing would fall in the extreme lower-left corner of love and freedom. Love abounded in our home, but so did freedom to play and explore, which sometime proved to be somewhat worrisome. Here is one good example.

In Albuquerque, we lived two blocks from Central Avenue, which was also the well-known Highway 66. On this avenue, about four blocks from our house, was the Lobo, a popular movie theater. When I was six years old, I would walk up to the theater and watch a movie. Only those over eight years old had to pay, so I would just walk in. One night my mother and father were going to a faculty party and told my older sister, Dodie, to look after me. This was a special time since I was to turn seven the next day, and I was going to have a big birthday party at my house.

Bill Junior as a youth

After my sister gave me supper, I went to my room, but I was so excited that I could not sleep. I then walked out of the house without telling anyone and decided to go up to the theater. They let me in as usual, and I went to the front and began to watch the movie. Since it was a romantic comedy, I was not very interested, so I lay down on the seats to watch. The next thing I knew, I woke up in the theater, but there was no movie on the screen, and the theater was dark except for the exit signs, which gave a slight hue so that I could see. I looked around and then shouted, "Is anyone here?" but there was no answer. I then ran out to the lobby and began to be afraid since the lobby area, which was usually brightly lit, was so dark. I ran to the front doors, but they were locked. I was trapped inside the theater. On several occasions I had used the telephone in the theater office, so I went there. I could not see the numbers on the dial, so I counted the holes on the dial pad and called my home. When Dodie answered the phone, I told her I was locked in the theater, but she would not believe me. She dropped the phone and ran to my room where I should have been, but it was empty. She told me to stay where I was and then she called my parents. Shortly after my call home, my parents met me at the front doors, but they could not get in and I could not get out. Soon several policemen came to the doors and then the firemen. I began to cry, and my parents wanted to know if I was afraid, but I told them I was concerned that I would miss my birthday party. It was to take place the next day at 10:00 a.m., and the theater did not open until 2:00 p.m. Well, after about a half hour the owner of the theater came with a key and let me out.

Poor Grades in School

One of God's great blessings to young children is that they do not understand the significance of making good grades, at least I did not. As children get older, their parents tell them enough times how important good grades are to encourage them to try harder. In elementary school, grades were not important to me. There were, however, two events that made me conscious that I was at the bottom of my class academically.

Pat Callahan was my best friend. His mother was a teacher in another school and always pushed Pat to make good grades. In our grade school the report cards had only one of three letters: "S" for satisfactory, "I" for improving, "U" for unsatisfactory. I always got all "I's" but not "U's" since the teachers liked me and knew I was trying. One time when we brought our grades home, Pat's mother saw his report card with all "S's" and mine with all "I's." She then made a joke about how I got straight "I's" and commented that the "I" was a straight letter, but her son got crooked "S's." Everyone laughed at her comment; however, for the first time I knew I was the low man on the totem pole as far as my performance in school was concerned.

On a second occasion the teacher was choosing students to be "Patrol Boys" for the school. Their job was to get to the main street crossings before school was out and stop the traffic so the students could cross the street safely. They wore a neat belt that ran across their waist and their chest and they held a great stop sign. Every time they chose the students for this job I was left out, so I asked the teacher why. She responded that only those with good grades could be patrol boys. At that time, I began to feel like I was missing something.

Every year in grade school the teacher would talk with my mother and suggest that I be held back a year since I was the youngest in the class and not doing all that well, and every year my parents would talk the teacher into letting me pass so that I could be with my friends. Doing so was possibly a mistake, but, nevertheless, I was always passed on to the next grade. I do not remember that did bothered me very much, but it was apparent that I was at the bottom of the class in scholastic achievement. Several teachers informed my mother that I was a good boy but could never go to college. This mediocrity continued into junior and senior high school.

In high school I came home with a lot of D's on my report card, but at the same time, I at least passed each class—except for Spanish. Because of my dyslexia, my memorizing skills were poor, and I simply could not learn another language. I failed Spanish in the fourth grade and again Spanish in my junior year of high school. My parents were concerned about my poor grades, but for mother they were not important, and my dad always said I would do better in college since that was what happened to him. My inability to learn a language followed me to my other schools. Again, the only course I failed in the university was German, and at seminary I always received the grade of D or D minus in Greek and Hebrew. Later I was able to become fluent in German, but I learned it like a small child learns how to speak, by interacting with those speaking the language daily, so after serving in German speaking Europe for thirty years, I had perfected my grasp of the language.

Learning How to Work and to Play Sports

It was true that I was not academically good in school, but my father taught me how to work at an early age. While I was still in junior high school, he started the Albuquerque Testing Laboratory (ATL), and I worked a minimum of fifteen hours a week in either the lab or in helping him construct the building for the lab. The only exception for working daily was when it came to sports. I always loved sports and played football and baseball whenever possible. If I had a game or wanted to practice, I could take time off from work. Sports were a priority for my dad, so he allowed me to indulge in my passion.

Every summer I went to the Elks picnic in the mountains close to Albuquerque. They had races for different age groups, and I always won all the races in my age group, which made my dad proud. Work and sports became an important part of my growing up experience, so much so that my poor grades did not seem to be so bad.

Chapter 2: Failure in School   25

Building up the Albuquerque Testing Laboratory

A Few Failures in Growing Up

As with any young person growing up in America today, there were some experiences that I wish I never had. In looking back, I can list at least three. The first one took place when I was in the sixth grade. My good friend was a very smart boy by the name of Sonny Montoya. (In Albuquerque we always had excellent relations with Hispanics and those of other minorities. I did not realize there could be problems until I got to the university.)

It was a warm summer evening, and we wanted to go up to the bowling alley and buy two banana splits. They cost twenty-five cents each, and we only had a dime. Sonny mentioned that the nearby bottling company had many cases of empty bottles out in the back yard behind a tall fence. If we could get a case out of the yard and take it to the store, they would give us two cents for each bottle, for a total of forty-eight cents. We could buy our desired treat. Thus, when it was dark, we went to the bottling company and began to climb the fence. We were about to the top when Sonny said, "We gotta get out fast." We ran and hid. Very soon a police car drove up, and the officer asked us what we were doing. After a short interview, the policeman took Sonny and me home to our parents. I remember well the policeman going to my door, knocking, and my father coming to the door. Dad was having a party with all his faculty members, and the policeman proceeded to tell him that his son was a thief and that he needed to take better care of me. At that time, I received my first and only spanking.

Another regrettable experience took place on a Sunday afternoon. The night before my parents had been hosting a party when the electricity went out. They had to continue the party using candles for light. Although I was not at the party, they told me about what had happened. That afternoon my parents took a nap, but I decided I wanted to see what it was like having only candles in the dark. I lit a candle, went into my closet with it, and closed the door. I then knew what it was like, but that was only the beginning of my new knowledge about fire. I remember barely touching one of my sweaters with the flame. I knew it caught fire, but I thought I had put it out. Several minutes later I went out to hit tennis balls against the garage door. The garage was next to my room. Smoke began to seep into the garage, so I went into my room, which was filled with smoke, and opened the closet door. I was met with a fireball. I ran and woke up my parents, and we tried to put out the fire with a hose, but soon the fire department came and extinguished the flame. Afterward, I had a little discussion with the fire chief.

About six months after the closet experience, my parents invited his Dean and his family over for Sunday lunch. It was July 5; we had enjoyed fireworks the day before. The dean's son was about my age, so I took him into a small back room in our garage where we lit some sparklers to continue our celebration. When we were finished, both of us left the garage and went out to play on the lawn. Suddenly, my father ran out of the house and into the garage to pull out the car. Smoke was billowing out of the garage. After retrieving the car, dad started to run back into the garage, shouting that his son was in there. At the last moment he looked up and saw me sitting on the grass. I had never seen such mixed emotions from him before. The garage was a total loss, and this time my discussion with the fire chief was a little bit more serious.

These experiences did not necessarily show that I was a bad boy, but they did reveal that I was one who had the capability of getting into trouble.

CHAPTER 3

Facts on Dyslexia

> "The greater the difficulty, the more glory
> in surmounting it. Skillful pilots gain their
> reputation from storms and tempests."
> – Epicurus

Definition

When I was a child doing poorly in school, the teachers would just say that I was not smart. Educators did not define each given weakness as they now do. I have learned that dyslexia is the first general term used to describe a variety of learning problems. Eventually, these problems were subdivided and categorized to describe different disabilities. In the early days, researchers felt that those with the weakness had experienced some form of nerve or brain damage. Others felt that it was just a congenital malfunction. In the 1920s one expert, Dr. Samuel Torrey Orton, redefined dyslexia as "cross lateralization of the brain." He said that this meant that the left side of the brain was doing what the right side was normally supposed to do, and the right side was doing the job of the left side. Many theories have been developed about the right and left sides of the brain and their functions. One author identifies dyslexia as the "Mother of Learning Disabilities." Today, over seventy terms are used to describe its various aspects.

In 2002 the Board of the International Dyslexia Association formally adopted the follow definition:

> "Dyslexia is a specific learning disability that is neurobiological in origin. It is characterized by difficulties with accurate and/or fluent word recognition and by poor spelling and decoding abilities. These difficulties typically result from a deficit in the phonological component of language that is often unexpected in relation to other cognitive abilities and the provision of effective classroom instruction. Secondary consequences may include problems in reading comprehension and reduced reading experience that can impede growth of vocabulary and background knowledge."

Many researchers in this field believe that human beings think in two different ways: verbal conceptualization and nonverbal conceptualization. Verbal conceptualization means thinking with the sounds of words, while nonverbal conceptualization means thinking with mental pictures. While I was at seminary, I was told that people learn in four different ways: (1) verbal (including reading), (2) visual, (3) practice, and (4) creative.

A person with dyslexia is always one who learns far more by the last three ways, but primary and secondary schools have traditionally emphasized verbal learning. With the current emphasis on technology and the availability of computers at all levels of school, those who learn visually are now being served much better since the nonverbal skills are being used more.

Symptoms

While I was growing up, I never heard the word dyslexia, and I doubt that my parents ever heard it either. We just did the best we could and did not give excuses for any failings that we had. Instead of blaming my poor grades on a congenital weakness, I just tried to do as well as I could and let the chips fall where they would. It was not until I went to the university and took a psychology course that I began to see things differently. I thought that the whole area of study of psychology was both interesting and challenging. As our professor described the various types of mental problems, I felt that with each problem he discussed, he was describing me, and most of my classmates felt the same. I came away from that class, not with solutions, but with the opinion that I was one big problem. Dyslexia was also mentioned, and the symptoms were outlined, and again I thought that must be me. I later learned that in most areas I was sane and healthy; thus, I forgot all the lectures I had in psychology. Dyslexia went the way of all the other neuroses. It was only after I had completed most of my schooling that I revisited the symptoms of dyslexia. It was then truly clear to me that I had lived with this weakness most of my life. What I had thought was just a lack of intelligence was really the roots of a well-defined problem with which I was living.

The symptoms of this complicated weakness vary according to age, but some general symptoms are common to most.

1. Talk later than most children. (I walked early and talked later).
2. Have difficulty pronouncing words, and when a mistake is made, not recognizing the mistake.
3. Confuse small words such as "at" and "to" and "goes" and "does."

4. Are weak in spelling.
5. Have an inability to memorize longer passages.
6. Confuse letters such as "e" and "i".
7. Read at a lower level than expected.
8. Avoid reading aloud.
9. Have difficulty in learning another language.
10. Words and letters sometimes jump around on the written page as one reads them.

Dyslexia can vary in intensity depending on many factors.

When I was a guest professor at a Southern Baptist seminary, I was talking with another professor about this topic, and he related an event that had recently happened to him with one of his students. This person's grades were incredibly low. But it appeared that he would graduate with his Master of Theology. In his last semester, this student was just barely making it in the course taught by the professor who was telling the story. The professor asked all the students to read a given two chapters in the Bible; they would then discuss it as a class. As they were reading, he walked around and observed the students. When he came to the student in question, he realized the student had his Bible upside down. The professor was furious and accused the student of not taking his request seriously, but then the student explained that he suffered from dyslexia and that one of his difficulties was that he could not read anything right side up. The book had to be upside down. Many who suffer a similar problem will begin books or newspapers at the back. I still read my newspapers from the back pages first and move forward.

Later in life I was filming a television interview. I had spoken on this channel several other times and had always been allowed to speak freely. The programs always went well; thus, I was invited back because I had no problems communicating. This time, however, they had written out what they wanted me to say and put it all on a teleprompter. They told me to just look into the camera; I would see in large red letters what I was to read. When I looked at the letters, however, they were jumping all around. I told them I could not read what was on the teleprompter, so they enlarged the type for me. The words and letters still seemed to be moving. After several tries and my pleading to let me just give the message without reading, they decided to cancel the taping. I still cannot use a teleprompter.

Famous People with Dyslexia

In the absence of good information on dyslexia, I thought that only losers suffered from this disability of not being able to read. As I studied further, I was amazed to learn that many great leaders who helped shaped history were dyslexic. Some whose names appear on this list were pioneers in the Western part of the U.S. while others were artists. A few were well known politicians or successful businesspeople. The following list is just a few of those who lived with this ailment but who still succeeded in life.

Hans Christian Andersen	Whoopi Goldberg
Henry Belafonte	William Lear
Alexander Graham Bell	Jay Leno
Richard Branson	George Patton
George Burns	Greg Louganis
Winston Churchill	Nelson Rockefeller
Leonardo da Vinci	Charles Schwab
Walt Disney	Jackie Stewart
Albert Einstein	Woodrow Wilson
F. Scott Fitzgerald	W. B. Yeats

The Weakness with a Plus

Having dyslexia does not mean that a person is dumb. Quite the contrary. Often it can be a gift if it is used in the right way. The mental function that causes dyslexia is a fight in the truest sense of the word, but it is also a natural ability, a talent that can be used to enhance the individual. Every person has been given certain gifts by God, and when one gift is weak, some other will gain strength, thus giving the person an advantage.

Most dyslexics share eight basic abilities.

1. They can utilize the brain's ability to alter and create perceptions.
2. They are highly aware of the environment
3. They are more curious than the average person.
4. They think mainly in pictures instead of words.
5. They are highly initiative and insightful.
6. They think and perceive multi-dimensionally (using all the senses).
7. They can experience thought as reality.
8. They have a vivid imagination.

As I first read thee eight abilities, I looked at my life and realized that many of these eight were really my strengths. Once again it became apparent hat the adage is true, "When God closes a door, He opens a window". My weaknesses were apparent but also, I had some hidden strengths that were seldom measured in the schools I attended.

Later in life when I realized I had dyslexia, I had to face one question: Would I have been better off knowing and understanding this weakness at an early age or was I better off just living my life as it came? I now think that I have been better off not learning about it when I was young. I did not use that as an excuse but rather just naturally began to use other talents and gift

CHAPTER 4

Formation and Development

> "When I was a child, I talked like a child, I thought like a child, I reasoned like a child. When I became a man I put childish ways behind me."
> – I Corinthians 13:11

My years in junior high school and the first two years of high school continued to show my weakness in school. They also showed me that I had some real problems in my social development. These years were filled with challenges, but at the same time, it was during this period that I began to develop as an adult who could live with my weaknesses.

Wanting to Be a Part of the "In" Group

Every school in America seems to have groups of students who are considered the "In" group. They are the popular kids. My junior high was no different. My problem was that I was not a part of that group. I would look at those kids who were popular and wish that someday I could be accepted as they were, but it was not yet time.

In this age of the Internet, gigantic problems are created when students use social media to run down fellow students or to ruin their reputations. When I was in junior high, we had a primitive, but just as effective, method to do the same. It was called "The Slam Book." Any student who wanted to have such a book would simply purchase a three-hole notebook at a store. The first page of the notebook was for the signatures of those who read the book or wrote something in it. At the top of every page in the notebook appeared the name of a student who was to be evaluated. The numbers of those signing in corresponded to the pages of those being evaluated, so it was possible to identify who was saying what. Often the students would describe a classmate as neat, beautiful, etc. In other cases, they would call them lazy, stupid, or some other negative descriptive term. My problem was that no one ever rated me because I was so far out from being accepted that my name was never even mentioned in any of the books. I was totally left out.

Young Evangelist Opens Revival Service Tonight

Bill Wagner Jr., 20, student evangelist, will open revival services at 7:30 tonight at the Girard Baptist Church, 1300 Girard Blvd. NE. Services will continue through Sunday.

Mr. Wagner, who will be a senior at the University this year, plans to attend a Baptist Theological seminary when he graduates.

Young peoples fellowship sessions and Bible discussions are scheduled each night in the youth conducted revival. The fellowship period is from 6 to 7 p.m. and the Bible work is scheduled from 7 to 7:30 p.m.

Sponsor Services

Juniors and intermediates, from 9 to 17 years, are sponsoring the services.

Leaders for the revivals include Jim Hilderbrand, song leader, a junior at Highland High; Tommy Edwards of Mountainair, pianist, who is a sophomore at the University of New Mexico.

Assisting will be Wayne Walraven of Sandia Base, Yvonne Herring of Albuquerque, who did summer missionary work in Phoenix, and Sally Crook of Albuquerque, who did summer missionary work in Hawaii. Miss Herring will be a sophomore at UNM and Miss Crook will be a senior at the University.

Testimonials

Miss Crook will show slides of Hawaii at the session.

Testimonials of faith will be given during the revival by Frances Kitchen, Louise Plemons, Gary Green, Jerry May-field, Danny Whitaker and Glen Smith.

Committee chairmen include Tommy Hough, publicity; Barbara Clark, visitation; Carolyn Morrow, refreshments; Kay Wentworth and Berry Belew, fellowship.

Bill Wagner Jr.

Bill Wagner begins his work in evangelism at an early age.

It was about this time that my male classmates began dating the girls. Generally, when I asked a girl out, she simply said no. One time Shirley, a cute classmate did accept my invitation to go to the "Holiday on Ice" with another couple and me. About 5:00 p.m. the night we were to go on the date, she called me and said she could not go. I knew how Charlie Brown felt in his courting of the little red-haired girl. I went by myself. My failure to go out with girls went all the way up through my sophomore year in high school. It was definite; I was not a member of the "In" group socially.

Trying to Be Successful in Music

In the second grade my friend Pat purchased a clarinet and joined the well-developed grade school band. I asked my mother if could do the same, and she agreed. In this band there were fifty who played the clarinet, and the beginners would take the last seats. As a person became better, he or she could challenge the person in front of him or her, and if successful, that student would move up a chair. Pat and I began at the back, in chairs forty-nine and fifty. After playing for five years, Pat had moved up to the second chair, but I had moved up only to chair forty-eight. Music simply was not my cup of tea. However, I was so self-confident that I asked the conductor if I could play a solo during the Saturday morning practice. Every week one student from the band would be selected to play a solo, and I wanted to try. The conductor granted my wish and said he would work with me in my preparations. We did not find the time to practice; nevertheless, I played the solo. I was later told that I had the worst solo every played in front of the band. I did not continue in band in junior high.

I was not, however, going to give up on music. In junior high they had Glee Club. My father was not happy that I took Glee Club as a course, but it was here that I felt I could succeed in music. As we were preparing for a big concert, the teacher approached me and told me that I was someone special and that she wanted me to be the one who arranged the chairs and made sure all the students had their music. I felt that I truly was someone special; only later did I learn that this assignment was her way of getting me out of performing since I was always off key. One problem that later became an asset was that I had a strong voice, and she wanted me out of choir because everybody could hear me. I lasted only one year in Glee Club. Even though I did take piano lessons (at the suggestion of my mother) and guitar lessons (wanting to be in a western band), I never excelled in the field of music.

Once again while being the pastor at Hermosa I was reminded that I was no musician. In the church our music director was a young man, Bill Whitworth. He was a good music director and generally a talented person. Because I enjoyed preaching so much, I was convinced that everyone could preach so I approached Bill and told him that he should preach sometimes. He told me that he could not preach. I insisted that he could. He then asked me if I would sing a solo at a church service. I told him that I could not sing, but he said that everyone can sing. We then made an agreement. In two weeks at the Sunday evening service I would sing a solo and he would preach. We pulled it off but two days after his event the board of deacons came to me and told me never to do that again. It was a disaster. I never sang a solo again.

Birthmark

One time my mother told me than when she first saw me in the hospital she cried because I was the ugliest baby she had ever seen. Later she denied ever making this remark, but I can imagine her reaction was correct because I have a very large birthmark that covers about one third of the right side of my face. Anyone who saw me immediately saw the birth mark. Surprisingly, it did not seem to bother me when I was growing up, but it could have been negative when others saw me. When we were attempting to be approved as missionaries, we had to visit a psychologist for about three hours. He asked me how my birthmark had affected me as a child and if it had given me an inferiority complex. I stated that I did not think so. He replied, "Oh yes. It did effect you as a child; it had to." I again answered, "It really did not bother me." He was insistent and said it had to have affected me negatively. Instead of arguing with him I agreed that it was a terrible blot on my life. He was now happy, and I was happy because he was happy, but the truth was that it never did bother me.

In my university days in Albuquerque, we had the anniversary of the foundation of our city and all the men grew beards for the celebration, so I joined in. I was amazed to notice that my beard covered all the birthmark. The beard line corresponded almost exactly with my birthmark. It seems as if this had been planned by God. Because I received many compliments on my beard, I decided to keep it. I still have it to this day.

Learning that Failure Can Lead to Success

It seemed that there was little that I could be good at, but I never gave up. While I was in junior high, my mother made a re-dedication of her life to Jesus Christ in the Seventh Day Adventist Church, and she began to take me to Sabbath School and church every Saturday (during this period in my life I worked or played sports on Sundays). Also attending the church was a student from the hated rival high school, Albuquerque High. This

Chapter 4: Formation and Development

student had a Letterman's sweater, which said to me that he was accepted. During church services I would look at that sweater and dream of the day I too could have such an honor. I continued to dream of accomplishing something great, yet even when I was looking to advance, I was not unhappy. My family and my friends kept me going, and I must admit that I had a rather happy childhood. I was not so preoccupied with success that I failed to enjoy all the good things I did have.

Even though it was a time when there were few victories, I could see that I was developing some parts of my personality that would later be helpful in my maturing as a person. Living in one neighborhood and going to the same schools helped me to develop a strong foundation for my future growth. My teachers all noticed my weakness in school and tried to help me achieve more. Again, I was fortunate in having teachers who were sympathetic and helpful. One even mentioned that she admired me because I at least tried to do better. My grades, however, still seemed to be at the bottom of the scale. Some might say that my period up to my junior year of high school was anything but successful, but I see that God was using my many friends and various activities in forming a foundation for my ministry many years later. God was good to me, and now I can see that He was leading me through these tough times.

Chapter 5

Football Success

> "Do you not know that in a race all the
> runners run, but only one gets the prize.
> Run is such a way as to get the prize."
> – I Corinthians 8:24

Until I entered my junior year in high school, nothing really changed. I was still poor in my academic side of school, I played football and made the freshman team but did not excel, and socially I was still not accepted. My relationship to God consisted of going to church off and on and sometimes to Sunday school (my mother had now become a Baptist), but there was no real spiritual commitment. The dreams of being a part of the "In" group persisted although this did not consume me. During my junior year, however, I was able to see my fortunes change for the better.

Running for Class Officer

Every year the students at my high school elected class officers, students who would serve for the entire year, and every year I thought about running for one of the offices. At the start of my junior year at Highland High School, I decided to at least try. Each class elected three officers: president, vice-president/treasurer, and secretary. I knew that I could not succeed in winning one of the first two offices, but I noticed that traditionally the class secretary was a girl. I learned that there were fifteen girls running for this office but no boys, so I entered the race for secretary of the junior class. Because the votes for the girls were split, I won. This new role helped me greatly in gaining acceptance.

Being Successful in Sports

Several people told me that I had lots of talent in sports. I was both fast and quick, but at 5'6" and 120 pounds, I was also the smallest one trying out for football. Because of my size, the coaches discouraged me, but again with my determination, I tried out anyway. That year I made the junior varsity, and we got to practice with the big boys (the varsity). One of our exercises was that the junior varsity players would act as blocking dummies for the varsity. We would get in a line and then run towards the more experienced varsity players. They would throw a body block and knock us down. I observed what was happening, and it occurred to me that every time one of the JV boys was blocked, even though he was not being hit hard, he would just collapse, and the blocker would seem to be successful I thought I would change this. I determined that the next time it was my turn, I would hit the blocker harder than he hit me. It worked. I was hit, but the blocker flew off me, and I continued to run. After I did this about three times, the coaches called the main coach for the varsity over to watch me. They then got our biggest and meanest player from the varsity and told him to block me. I ran towards him with the determination to hit him harder that he hit me, and it worked again. I had made an impression. The only problem was that the coach thought that a player with my ability to hit hard together with my speed meant that I should become a blocking guard. A lineman at my size? That idea did not work, and by the end of the season I was changed back to halfback.

By the start of my senior year, I felt like I had arrived. I was one of the starting halfbacks on our team. The other halfback, Tommy McDonald, received a scholarship to play for the University of Oklahoma. He turned pro and played with the Philadelphia Eagles and eventually made the NFL Hall of fame. Our team was good, and we went on to take second place in the state of New Mexico. Our last game was against our great foes, the Albuquerque High School Bulldogs. It was supposed to be a close game, but we won, and I scored two touchdowns. After the game, the coach gave me the game ball as a measure of my success. Being on the football team gave me a high profile in the school.

At the beginning of my junior year, my dad wanted me to go out for track. Although I was fast, the school track team had several students who were faster in the 100-yard race. Since my dad had run the 440 yards in college, he told me to go out for it. I went to the coach and told him of my desire. He asked if I had ever run that distance before, and my reply was a strong no. He said, "Okay, run 440 yards for me." Without any preparation, I did what he said. Afterward he said he thought he could help me develop into a 440-yard runner. I was also good in the long jump, and since I had a lot of speed, he put me on both the low and the high hurdles. I did not achieve much in track my junior year, but by my senior year I was one of the stars on the state champion track team, and at the state track meet I scored two gold medals and two fourth places in the hurdles. Once again, I had achieved my goals in sports.

Since football was in the fall and track was in the spring, I had nothing to do during the winter months, so I tried out for the wrestling team. This Sport was new in my school at that time, but I made the team, and my senior year I became the captain of the wrestling team. By the end of my senior year, I had earned that much covered Letterman's sweater, excelling in football, track, and wrestling. Sports had been good to me.

Forming the Dirty Eight

By the beginning of my senior year in high school I was somewhat well known, and most people would have been happy with these achievements, but I still saw a mountain to climb. I wanted not only to be accepted but rather to excel in popularity. Another possibility came my way – the creation of the Dirty Eight.

Seldom has any one group of students so completely dominated the social, political, and daily life of a high school as did the Dirty Eight at Highland High in Albuquerque. This achievement was no simple matter since the school was the largest in the state of New Mexico with over 2500 students. This accomplishment was not planned but was just accidental. It started prior to my senior year, with a small band of boys who began to run around with each other, and it soon became apparent that this eight had formed a clique.

One night at the start of the school year, eight of us decided to organize a club. We considered many names, but finally the "The Dirty Eight" was presented. It had no real meaning, especially since all the fellows came from middle class homes and none of us were lacking in morals or in cleanliness. It was a simple thing. The guys just wanted a different name, and here it was: "The Dirty Eight" was born. There was no written purpose for the club, no constitution, no officers, no regular meeting times, and no rules, but we did stick together; the name itself was the only force that gave us cohesion.

Early in the school year, the various members of the group began to run for school offices. One became the president of the student body, and I was elected the first vice president. The only office in the Student Council that was denied to us was that of secretary-treasurer. That position went to a girl, and, of course, girls were not allowed to be a member of the Dirty Eight. One member was elected president of the Letterman's club and another became the president of the Honor Society. One after the other, the elective offices went to one of our members. It appeared as if the Dirty Eight had arrived.

About halfway through the year, four other boys wanted to join the group. Each of the four was a proven leader; therefore, we changed the name to match the new members. We were now the "Dirty Eight Plus Four." We continued to dominate the school. Soon after the name change, the principal called us twelve boys into his office to talk. "Boys," he said in his strong but pleasing manner, "I know that you are proud of your organization, but don't you think that you could help the school more by disbanding the Dirty Eight? It has been brought to my attention that you have formed a clique and that some of the students and teachers are complaining about it." This comment really made us think since the last thing we wanted to do was to harm our beloved school. We promised the principle that we would think about it and see what could be done. That night we met to talk. In the end, we decided that the Dirty Eight would not disband. We were convinced that we were not harming the school in any way and that our existence did just the opposite. It gave the school the leadership that it needed. Little was said after that, and the club continued to the end of the school year. That year the biggest social event in the school was not the Junior-Senior Ball but rather the Dirty Eight Ball.

By the end of the school year I was happy with my successes. In fact, one of the top girls in the school asked me, "How is it that you, being one of the school's biggest nerds the first two years, can now be one of the neatest kids on campus?" I did not have an answer for her, but now I was on top of the world. I even had a girlfriend who I thought I loved and wanted to marry. Mariel was both beautiful and smart. In fact, she was elected to be one of the two homecoming princesses. For me, life at that point was worth living.

Facing Reality

The only person who really knew how I felt at that time was myself, and I was having a hard time trying to convince myself that everything was going well. Some days as I came home from a party or being with Mariel, I would walk on the street close to my house and think. My life was like a large jigsaw puzzle that had all the pieces in place except the one in the middle that was missing. Truthfully, my life was incomplete despise my successes. I thought that maybe after I got married, I would find that piece or maybe it was waiting for me at the university I was going to attend. One thought was that if I left home and became 100 percent free of my parents, that would bring me my middle piece.

Chapter 5: Football Success

I was relatively certain that the missing piece was not religion. After all, I had been a member of several Sunday schools. At one time or another I had regularly attended the Sunday schools of the Lutherans, Methodists, Presbyterians, Christian, and Seventh Day Adventists. My senior year in high school found me attending a little Baptist church down the street from my house. For me, religion was not the answer although I did sometimes think about my relationship to God. Once I attended a revival at the little church, and during the invitation at the end of the sermon, the preacher said that he wanted all those in the audience who knew they would go to heaven if they died to raise their hand. I raised my hand, but I felt like a ton of bricks was tied to it. This experience caused me to think more about my relationship to God.

All in all, I had succeeded. I was where I wanted to be, but no way could I have predicted the path that God was leading me to take. During the summer of 1953, my life was radically changed.

CHAPTER 6

Faith in Christ

> "Remember now thy Creator in the days
> of thy youth, while the evil days come not."
> – Ecclesiastes 12:1

My Conversion to Christ

The summer after high school went well. I worked at the ALT and made good money, Mariel and I were getting along great, and I still had all my friends. In early summer, however, I began to see that the missing piece in my life was God. My mother wanted me to go to church with her, but I always found excuses why I could not go, and when I did go, the Holy Spirit would talk with me and show me my need to make a real commitment to Christ. When the invitation was given after every sermon, I rejected going forward, trying to convince myself that I was good enough and did not need to go further. The Holy Spirit, however, would not let go of me, and my thoughts often went to my need for a closer walk with Jesus Christ.

My feelings finally came to a point of decision late in the summer of 1953. One Friday night four of us were going to a movie. I was driving, and we went to pick up the last one of the group. We arrived at Ron's house a little early because we knew he was always late. The other two went in to get him, and they stayed inside waiting for him for about twenty minutes. I stayed in the car, where for some reason I had a religious program on the radio. The speaker said that if I wanted to know Christ, all I needed to do was to bow my head and accept Him as my Savior. In the car, while I was waiting for my friends, I bowed my head and gave my life to Christ. I have no doubts that this was the first time that I really knew what it meant to be saved. Jesus had truly come into my life. At that point there were no real changes in my life, but now my goals began to be quite different. I still wanted to marry Mariel and go to the University, but now Jesus began to take first place in my life.

Life at the University

As I said before, not much changed in my immediate circumstances. I was still living in the world; however, the Lord began to change my life is some unexpected ways. First was my relationship with Mariel. When I went to college, I was taken aback by the large number of cute little co-eds, so I suggested to Mariel that for a period we would date others, but she would still be my main girl. This idea did not set well with her, and she broke up with me. I thought this break was just temporary, so I dated a few other girls but then wanted Mariel to come back to me. She said no, and she meant it. I kept trying to change her mind, but to her I was nothing more than a past boyfriend. I remember going to the park and crying and begging God to have Mariel come back to me. I wanted to marry her, and I thought I could not live without her. I am so happy that God did not answer that prayer. That is often the way it goes. God knows better what is best for us. Anyway, for me Mariel was now out of the picture.

My next adventure was joining a fraternity. This step was the thing for all the "successful" students to do; thus, I went through rush and got invitations to join from all the fraternities, but I chose Sigma Alpha Epsilon since it was one of the two most prestigious on campus. It was great having fellowship with all the guys in the frat, and our meetings with various sororities were a step up, but all the time I could see that life in a fraternity was not really for a Christian. Neither the morals the members exhibited, nor the structure of the SAE frat supported my belief in Christ. I became a full member, but my heart was not really in the group.

At the university I continued with my sports, seeing them as a chance to gain status. I went out for football as a no scholarship walk on and made the freshman team. At that time freshmen were not allowed to play on the varsity team. I became the second-string halfback and played in all the games. An interesting point is that in high school the other halfback went on to be a NFL Hall of Fame football player while in the University the other halfback was Jerry Apodaca, who later became the Governor of New Mexico. I seemed to always be the other halfback.

Prior to that year I had never been hurt, but at one practice I attempted to tackle the biggest and meanest varsity running back. I hit him and bounced off the front of him. In those days we did not wear face masks, and he stepped right on my face. One of his cleats went right where my two front teeth had been. When I got up, the teeth were gone. The other three cleats left visible marks on my face. This injury slowed me down for part of the year, but I finished the year suffering no other injuries except for some concussions. By my sophomore year I had made

Chapter 6: Faith in Christ

the varsity team. My job was to be a running back and to run back punts. Again, my only injuries were some concussions. I was told that I was the smallest player in the nation in division I varsity football; I weighed only 142 pounds. Just being on the team gave me some desired status.

My football career at the university came to an end for two reasons. The first had to do with the final game of the season for the Lobos. Up to that game we had a five win and five loss record and wanted to win the last game so that we would have a winning season. We were playing the San Jose Spartans on their home field. Towards the end of the game, we were only four points behind, our defense had stopped them, and they had to punt. I was called on to return the punt. I remember well seeing the punt, which was a little short, coming down to me. Out of the corner of my eye I saw a large San Jose tackle coming towards me. The ball hit my chest and bounced into his arms. He ran for a touchdown, and we lost the game. I think that sealed the end of my football career. The second reason I quit was that the coach took me to a brain specialist, and he stated after testing me that because of the many concussions (ten in number) that I had experienced playing football, small blood clots were forming in the front of my brain. Both the coach and the doctor recommended that I stop playing. I took their advice. I did, however, continue with track and lettered in it before also giving that up due to a lack of time.

Living for Christ at the University

In Christ I had found the centerpiece of the puzzle, but this completion did not make life easy. It is not a simple matter living the Christian life at a secular university. There are multiple temptations as well as many barriers for the Christian. I experienced them all, but God knows that it is always easier when a young believer has help. God gave me the person I needed to guide me.

I first meet Sally Crook, who was later to become my wife, in the summer of 1953, before beginning college. I will say more about her later, but I want to note here that she gave me the help I needed in growing in my faith. What I knew about Sally was that she was a vibrant Christian who attended a Baptist church and lived her faith. She was greatly respected in her school for her faith and strong moral code. At that time, I was still going with Mariel, but I was impressed with Sally.

On the university campus was a building that housed the Baptist Student Union. I was afraid to go there, but finally in the middle of my first year, I went in. All the young people were Christians, but they were not especially those of the "In" group; however, I did see Sally there. Our friendship began to grow.

During the first part of my freshmen year I dated Gale, a Kappa-Kappa-Gamma girl. She was a lot of fun, and I enjoyed her company, and she was also a great dancer, which presented a problem for me. When I became a Christian, my pastor, Rev. Stan Unruh, gave me a list of things that a Christian did not do. This list included drinking, smoking, taking drugs, wearing a beard, and dancing. Since I had never done most of those things, they were not a problem. I did dance sometimes, but since I was not good at it, giving it up was no problem. Now I was dating Gale, and she was a great dancer, so we would go out dancing. Before I got on the dance floor, I would look around to see if Brother Unruh was looking and then dance if I did not see him. Gale and I really got together with the dance, and soon we became so good that when we danced, others would stop and watch us. It was more acrobatics than dancing, but we were good. Now I enjoyed dancing. Later, mainly because of my desire to go with Sally, Gale and I broke up. I also made a commitment not to dance again since I felt it hampered my Christian witness.

After my breakup with Gale, I was at the SAE frat house where we were entertaining Gale's sorority. I was standing with a group of the guys and girls when Gale came running up to me. "Bill, it's great to see you again." she said. "Let's dance." All the others who were standing with us thought it was a great idea. I told her no, and then she came right up to my face and said, "Bill Wagner, why will you not dance with me?" I swallowed hard and said, "I have made a commitment to Jesus Christ not to dance again." Gale turned and walked away, and one by one all the others excused themselves until I was alone. As I look back on this experience, I realize the importance of my commitment to God. Had I said I could not dance because Brother Unruh would not allow it, it would have seemed very lame. Refusing to dance became important to me not because I was told not to, but because I had made a commitment to God not to dance.

Sally Crook's Influence

Mariel was in the past, Gale was no longer on the scene, and a few other girls I had dated were totally unimportant, but I was greatly impressed with the now university cheerleader Sally Crook. I was not impressed with her last name, but I was assured that it did not have to do with her family's occupation but rather in England it had to do with a crook in the river or a crook in the back of a family member. I finally asked her to go out. On the day we were to have our first date, I took a nap and woke up about an hour before time to pick her up. I was still half asleep and wanted to call and break the date, but I went anyway. The rest is history. Her faith in Christ, together with her beauty, sold me on her. She was the right girl for me. We kept dating, and later I put my SAE pin on her; at that time doing so was the equivalent of a pre-engagement. For about two and a half years we were steady partners. Her faith was a great help in keeping my faith strong. I think that God used both of us to give strength to each other.

In our senior year we decided to get married. Sally wanted to be sure that she could finish her degree, so we waited until Thanksgiving our senior year to get married. We had a problem. Both of us had many friends in Albuquerque and she thought that we needed to invite all of them to the wedding. This meant a large wedding, one that her parents could not afford. We made the decision to have the smallest wedding possible, so when we married the night before Thanksgiving in 1956 there were only ten people present. Charles, a member of our church, said that as a wedding gift he wanted to be the photographer for the wedding. We agreed. He took many photos but two weeks later he informed us that his camera was broken and thus we have zero photos of our wedding. As we look back, we feel that this was a positive way to begin, not to look at the past but to look at the future.

At the university I wanted to know as much about God as possible, so I took courses at the BSU that helped to form my belief system. I also took the only course at the university that dealt with religion: World Religions. I remember well the professor stating that all religions were good except for Christianity, which really was two religions; one was the religion of Jesus and the other was the religion of Paul. People had to choose which one they preferred. The teachers at the University of New Mexico were no help in the process of developing my faith.

Surrendering to Preach

It may sound strange after all I have written to say that one of my biggest faults was that I was very, very shy, but it is true. It was always difficult for me to step out in front of others. This personality trait became a stumbling block for me when God called me to preach. After I had been a Christian for six months, God spoke to me, and I knew that He wanted me to preach the Gospel. The problem was that in our church, each person had to go forward at the invitation given at the close of the sermon, to tell the pastor what type of decision he or she was making. If I wanted to preach, I needed to walk to the front of the auditorium and tell Brother

Unruh that God was calling me into the ministry. I could not do it. Week after week I refused, mainly because of my shyness. Finally, one Sunday night during the invitation, I walked forward and took the pastor by the hand and announced that God had called me to preach. His response surprised me. "Bill" he said," the whole church has been aware of God's call to you." Then he asked me, "When do you want to preach your first sermon?" I replied, "In about four years." He replied, "I want you to preach in three weeks at the evening service." "Impossible," I said, but in three weeks I preached my first sermon. My text was Matthew 17:20: "Because you have so little faith. I tell you the truth, if you have faith as small as a mustard seed, you can say to this mountain, move from here to there and it will move. Nothing will be impossible for you." At that time in my life I needed all the faith I could gather. After the sermon, many came and told me it was not too bad. The minister then approached me and asked when I wanted to preach again, and I said, "In about four years." He gave me another three weeks.

In preparing for my second sermon, I studied and had most of it written out. Since I was to preach at 7:00 p.m. on Sunday evening, I went an hour early. On the side of the auditorium, where I preached, were two small rooms. At 6:00 p.m. I went into one of the rooms to do my last preparations. Brother Unruh knocked on the door at 7:00 and said it was time. I grabbed my Bible and came out and sat on the stage looking at all who had come. The pastor introduced me, and then it was my turn. I stood up and opened my Bible, only to I discover that I had left my outline and the written sermon on the table in the next room. What was I to do? Should I tell the people I needed to go get my sermon or should I say I could not preach? I said, "Let's pray," and then I preached without my notes. In that experience I discovered a wonderful lesson—when God calls you to preach about Him, He will be with you and give you the words to say. It was a learning experience.

Youth Revival movement

In the latter half of the 1940's a movement was started at Baylor University in Waco, Texas. As the story goes, a group of students had a great burden for the other students and for the citizens of Waco. They began to pray for direction as how best to reach out to those for whom they were praying. They felt that God directed them to hold a citywide revival in a rented auditorium in the city. They were not sure who they should invite to preach and lead the music, but the Lord told them that they were supposed to do these tasks. It was reported that seven of the young men

Chapter 6: Faith in Christ

were asked to preach one night each and another was to lead the music. Others would support them in many other ways including prayer meetings. The revival was a great success and the young men went out to churches in Texas to preach what was called Youth Revivals.

In our senior year of high school, Larry Walker, a close high school friend of Sally's, had such a team. Larry was the son of a Baptist minister in the city and was an outstanding leader in his school. Sally was the secretary for the team that Larry put together and she traveled around the Southwest on that team. After I surrendered to preach, I also formed a team, and we went to various churches in New Mexico to hold revivals. God used that time to help me develop my preaching skills. All over the southwest young people were called to preach the gospel. In time, many of the leaders of the Southern Baptist Convention were the same young people who were involved in the Youth Revival Movement.

During my time preaching in various churches, I had many special spiritual experiences. One took place in Albuquerque. As a student at the University of New Mexico, I had a burden for the other students, and I wanted to find a way to win them to Christ. At that time tent revivals were extremely popular. My plan consisted of locating an empty piece of land close to the university, renting a large tent, get some sawdust for the floor covering, chairs, a pulpit, lights, a generator, and a piano. I was going to hold a campus wide revival meeting. I did a lot of planning.

About three months before the revival was to begin, the First Baptist Church of Albuquerque had invited a famous Evangelist to come to the church for a revival. His name was Angel Martinez. Angel was a great preacher but was a little too flashy for my blood. He wore pink and purple suits and his preaching was rather flamboyant. But still I greatly respected him because he was truly a man of God. After one of the services I asked him if I could speak with him and he agreed that after the service we could meet.

At the meeting he listened patiently as I outlined my plans for the revival at the university. When I finished, he told me that the plans were good but that I forgot one thing. I thought, what could it be? Possibly a program, ushers, song book, etc. I asked him what had I forgotten? He then said "Bill first you need to go into your own bedroom with a piece of chalk. On the floor draw a big circle, then get down on your knees in the circle and pray that the revival would begin in that circle" I never forgot this advice. If I was to be a leader, I first must be sure that my own life was right with my Lord.

Albuquerque Rescue Mission

Also, in Albuquerque there was a rescue mission on First Street, in the bad part of town. I would go down there about once a week to preach to the down and outers. Again, this was great practice for my preaching. Many of those who came for a dinner and a place to sleep, accepted Christ. At one time I had three pistols at home that were given to me by those who had committed their lives to God, and they wanted me to keep them for safety. I remember that one night a large Hispanic man came forward to accept Christ. I spend over an hour talking with him. Later I was told he was one of the leaders of a bad gang. He invited me to go home with him that night. I remember well traveling to the poorer section of the city to a rundown shack. I went into the small house with the man. When we entered, He called out to his mother. "Mom it's me and I have brought home friend I want you to meet". She replied "I don't want to meet any of your friends. They are all bad people." "No, Ma, this one is a preacher". She came out and we spoke, and she cried for joy at the change in her son. The rescue mission was a great blessing for my life.

The Baptist Student Union

The Baptist Student Union (BSU) on the campus was also a great help in my development in the early stages of my Christian life. It was important for me to have a place to come every day for noonday devotions. Both Sally and I eventually took over leadership positions with me becoming the president of the New Mexico State BSU program. At the center I learned both how better to lead young people and to do administration work. Also, at the center I was able to take my first courses in Bible and theology that was offered by the head of the Student Department for the Baptists of New Mexico

The last two years of my university experience was different from the first two years and from my high school years. My main purpose in life was no longer to be popular but rather to make Jesus Christ popular. I was disappointed that some of my old friends were not interested in finding out more about how to serve God. They remained my friends but were not concerned about spiritual matters. Once I graduated, I was ready for the next important decision in life, that being how could I best serve my Lord.

CHAPTER 7

Father's Inspiration

"A man cannot have a better legacy to the
world than a well-educated family."
– Thomas Scott

Even though my father's tendency was to give me freedom, he still was an important influence on my life. My poor grades never pleased him, but it was his theory that as I grew older, I would mature, and the better grades would come. He even felt that it would be good for me to spend between two to four years in the military. As a professor during the Second World War, he had noticed that those students who left to serve in the military and then returned to school always made better grades. He had also learned a little proverb that he would often quote to me:

"Those who make the A's make the professors,
Those who make the B's make the judges, and
Those who make the C's make the money."

He strongly believed in the truth of this little saying, which helped me because in the university I was a "C" student. I remember well the time when I thought I had done well on a chemistry test only to learn that I had failed it with one of the lowest grades in the class. I came home, discouraged, and told my father that I wanted to join the army. He got his car and was ready to drive me down to the recruiting office. I quickly changed my mind and later barely passed chemistry.

Learning How to Get Better Grades

Even in college I was the slowest reader in class, and this hampered me in the social sciences, but it was not a hindrance in engineering and math. I was told that the American president could read many books every week by speed reading. It was a system by which the reader would look at only the first sentences of a paragraph or scan the book to find the most important ideas. I learned how to do this with some success. I seldom read the complete book, but I was still able to master most of the important teachings of the book. In this way I was able to get through many of the first- and second-year courses.

My dad had also made a study of how professors give tests. He taught me how to take tests to optimize my success. By just learning how a professor gives and grades a test, a person can do much better and get more positive results. When I had a problem course, he would take the time to sit down with me and help me learn the important aspects that I needed. It was a help in the civil engineering courses that he was the head of the department and all the teachers were under him. He knew them personally as well as knowing the material. He was truly a great help. Eventually the day came when I received my bachelor's degree in civil engineering. I also passed an important test called the EIT (Engineering in Training) that I needed as the first step in obtaining a license in the state to practice as an engineer. After five year of experience I also passed the larger test that gave me permission to practice as a licensed engineer in New Mexico. Dad was happy when I finally passed that last hurdle.

Encountering Two Major Problems

In my last two years at the university, I ran into two major problems that really needed to be solved. The first had to do with my call to serve God. In our family there were three children, my older sister Dodie, and Loretta, my younger sister, and myself. Dad was set on at least one of his children becoming an engineer. Dodie tried for a year, but she just was not the engineering type, so she quit. Loretta was totally deaf from having the measles when she was nine months old, so she could not be the engineer. That meant that I was the chosen one. My first two years at the University, all went well. I got through my general education classes, and in my junior year I could finally concentrate on just civil engineering courses, but I still had a problem. God, my heavenly father, had called me to preach while my earthly father wanted me to be an engineer. I approached my dad about switching to another field that would better prepare me for the ministry. To put it bluntly, he was not pleased. The problem was very great for me. To which of my two fathers should I listen?

Albuquerque was only about 80 miles from Glorieta Conference Center, a large Southern Baptist training facility, and many of the outstanding teachers in Southern Baptist circles would attend special emphasis weeks there. I heard that the famous biblical ethicist, Dr. T. B. Matson of Southwestern Baptist Seminary, was going to be teaching. I contacted him and got an appointment to discuss my situation. I explained my problem to him although I already felt that the answer must be that I

Chapter 7: Father's Inspiration

must first obey my heavenly father. In my discussion with him I presented my two options and asked for his advice. He asked me, "What does the Bible teach?" I replied, "It teaches a lot, but what do you mean." "What does the Bible say about your relationship to your parents?" He went on to say that the Bible says that we are to obey our parents. "But if I do this, I might not go into the ministry," I said. "Don't you think God knows that and don't you think God is on top of this situation? You need to obey your earthly father." This answer was not the one I expected, but I was ready to be obedient to my earthly father. I went home from Glorieta and told my dad, "I will continue in engineering if that is what you want." He then asked me when I would go to seminary, and I told him that I first needed a bachelor's degree, but the seminary wouldn't, at that time, accept an engineering degree for entrance. He then told me that he would pay for the extra year of university that I needed to get more social science courses and he would also help me go to seminary after I got my engineering degree. I now see that Dr. Matson was used by God to solve the problem.

Father teaching son how to be an engineer at an early age

My second problem was just as serious; it was between Sally and me. She strongly felt that she had been called by God to be a foreign missionary while I felt just as strongly that God had called me to be a minister in a church here in the States. Several times we were almost ready to break up since neither of us could deny our calling. God, however, gave us the answer.

During our junior year at the university, we began to make plans for the coming summer. Sally suggested that we go to the Southern Baptist Conference center in Ridgecrest, North Carolina, to work on staff. This idea did not appeal to me since I wanted to stay and work at the ATL. She told me how great it would be for us to be together in the green mountains of North Carolina for the whole summer. She convinced me, so we both applied to work on staff for the summer. Our plans were set, and I was truly looking forward to being with Sally there. Before we were to go, however, Sally came to me and said that unbeknownst to me, she had also applied for the new BSU mission program to go as a summer missionary to Hawaii, and she had been accepted. That meant that she was going to Hawaii while l was going alone to North Carolina. I was not happy but made the decision to go to Ridgecrest anyway.

My time in the good old South was truly inspiring, and one night during the Foreign Missions Week I was deeply touched by God and I felt a definite call to also go on the mission field. After that experience, I called Sally and my parents by long distance to tell them of this call to be a missionary. I was overly excited. At that time, I felt the place that I could best serve was Africa, but that was not to be. The second problem had now been solved, and that paved the way for us to get married. In the spring of 1957, we both graduated with bachelor's degrees. I then had to go to school for another year to satisfy the requirements for seminary. It was a good year, and I learned a lot. That year was financed by my father. I also worked full time at the Laboratory to gain needed experience so that I could take the test to get my license. During that year Sally became a high school History teacher and got the necessary experience she needed. We rejoiced as to how God had led us both.

Moving to Switzerland

At a world mission conference in Nashville at Christmas time 1956, we learned about a new Baptist seminary in Rüschlikon, Switzerland. We spoke to one of the professors about doing some of our seminary training there, and he told us that they accepted only a limited number of American students. We needed to get a recommendation from one of the leaders of the Foreign Mission Board to apply. The next summer we went to the Foreign Mission Week in Glorieta and spoke with several of the top leaders, but each one said that it was best for us to stay in the States for our studies. During the week Sally met the missionary she had worked with in Hawaii, and she told her she was excited about this possibility. A good friend of hers, Dr. Saddler, was the Secretary for Europe. He was the one who had created Rüschlikon. Based upon the recommendation from Sally's missionary friend, he agreed to recommend us to study there for our first year. We applied and kept up correspondence with the school

Chapter 7: Father's Inspiration

for about six months, and then we received a letter that said the school would probably not accept any students from America for the next year. We were discouraged and ready to stay in the States, but one day a letter came from Switzerland informing us that we had been accepted to begin our studies in the fall of 1958. My dad was willing to help us finance the trip. Again, we saw God working.

Sally and I went to Switzerland, and settled in at Rüschlikon, which was in an old estate overlooking Lake Zurich. The school was all one could ask for. We had supper with the president, Dr. Joseph Nordenhaus on the first night we were there. There were forty students from twelve countries and ten professors. The classes were small and the fellowship very international.

Coming from the desert of New Mexico, we were really taken aback by the beauty of Switzerland. In fact, when Sally returned to Albuquerque after being in Switzerland for a year, she asked her mother, who picked her up at the airport, when they had cut down all the trees. Her mother replied, "Sally, there never were trees in this part of Albuquerque." Our year in Switzerland was great, and we grew in many ways. The most important part was that now both Sally and I could see that our place of service could easily be central Europe. It was apparent to us that God had led us there at that time. After our first year we wanted to attend for another year, but we felt it far better for us to return and go to Southwestern Baptist Theological Seminary in Ft. Worth. It also had much to offer.

Chapel at Rüschlikon, Switzerland

Developing my Theology

As stated, our time in Rüschlikon was one of the best years of our lives. For the first time I could dedicate all my efforts to the study of the Bible and thus prepare myself for His service. Because of the very personal interest that most of our professors had in their students, I did rather well in most of my classes. Again, it was a language that was my worst area of study. In my Greek class we had four students', two Germans and two Americans. One of the Students, Wiard Popkes, who later became professor of Greek at the Hamburg Seminary, was an outstanding student and always made A's in the class. The other German was not interested in studying and always flunked the course. The two American students made D minus both semesters. The professor did all he could do to help the three weaker students. And that was probably the only reason I passed. Thus, I did get credit for passing Greek.

I must admit that I was not prepared to study in a European based theological seminary. The mode of the day in theology was the emphasis on historical and literary criticism. This means that nothing in the Bible was taken for granted. Everything was questioned. I came from a background where I believed that If the Bible said it, it was true, so now I had a real conflict. How do I deal with this immense criticism of the Bible while keeling my faith? During this year it was a problem.

Finally, I made a decision. It was in my Introduction to Old Testament class when we began the study of the book of Daniel. The professor was attempting to give a possible date for it being written. He said it was either about 607 B.C. or in the first century B.C. He said that he believed that it had to the later date because the prophecies had been so exact and that it had to be written after the fact and not before. This bothered me. My question was – Did God not prophesy the future through Daniel? This cause me to think for myself and from that point on I did not just take what the professor said but began to determine right from wrong based upon my acceptance of the Bible as the Word of God. This helped me to form my present day biblical based theology. The professors did not always agree with me but were helpful as I struggled to find the truth that I was looking for. From a theological standpoint my time in Switzerland prepared me for both my next years of study at the conservative Southwestern Baptist Seminary and for my service in Europe as a missionary.

Chapter 7: Father's Inspiration

Moving to Texas

In Ft. Worth Sally taught in one of the high schools to help support us. I also got a part time job with an engineering firm, which again helped me to get the required five years of experience before I could take the test to get a license. Southwestern was different from Rüschlikon. It had three thousand students, which meant that the students seldom got to know their teachers. Dr. Naylor, the president was a fine man. I shook his hand on the first day and again at gradation. That was the limit of my contact with the president. Still I received a great education. We found a good church and lived a quiet but busy life. Again, my grades were not stellar, especially in Greek and Hebrew, but they were better than in the university. In order to graduate in two years, I had to attend summer school in 1961. That year Sally informed me that we were expecting our first child. We had waited to get married until we were practically finished with the University so that Sally could finish before we began our family. Now we wanted a child, and it was just a coincidence that the due date was the exact day of my graduation from seminary. Talk about family planning.

Facing Another Disappointment

While preparing for the ministry, I was told of the great need for both student workers and ministers, so I expected that many would want my services when I graduated. After all, I needed to have two years of ministry experience before we could be appointed as missionaries. I remember being shocked at our gradation practice. Dr. Naylor asked all the graduating students who had a place to serve at that time to raise their hand. Only about 20 percent of the hands went up. I was one of the ones who had nowhere to go. I asked, "What about me"?

We returned to New Mexico, and I went to the state office of the New Mexico Baptists seeking help in finding a place of ministry. I was told that at that time there was only one church looking for a pastor, and they had over one hundred applicants. There was no need for BSU workers in the whole Southern Baptist convention that year. I felt my studies were useless, so we made the decision to stay in Albuquerque. I worked again for the Albuquerque Testing Laboratory.

Two weeks after I graduated, Candice, our first child, was born. We bought a house and began life anew in Albuquerque. Shortly after getting settled, I heard that a small group from an established church had rented a closed "Seven-Eleven" store and wanted to start a church. Most of those from the bigger church were against a new mission, but those who were already meeting decided to go ahead anyway. Soon after they started, they asked me to preach. They liked what they heard. Although they could not pay me anything, they would let me preach every week. I accepted their invitation; this small group was the beginning of Hermosa Drive Baptist Church. We stayed there for four years, and during this time my position moved from no salary to part time to full time. We had three building projects, and after the four years we had over 400 members. Many were from university sport teams. God truly blessed this ministry.

Remembering Two Events at Hermosa

Two notable events occurred while I was pastor at Hermosa Drive. One was happy, and the other was hard. I will start with the hard one. After we had been there for two years and were well settled in the church, I had a pain in my side on a Tuesday night. On Wednesday I visited one doctor who said it was just indigestion and not to worry. On Wednesday night I led the prayer meeting while leaning on the pulpit because of the pain. Someone gave me the name of another doctor, a surgeon. When I called him, he asked me, while I was on the phone, to do several activities, such as put my right leg over my left leg and then the reverse. After about five questions, he told me that I had appendicitis and I should go immediately to the hospital where he would meet me. They rolled me into surgery, and afterward the doctor told Sally that everything was all right. The appendix had some infection, but they got it all. We were relieved. I stayed in the hospital for several days but still had a great deal of pain at the location of the incision. The doctor said that some people have a high threshold of pain and others a lower one. He told me not worry.

On Friday he let me go home. That night and all the way into Saturday the pain was bad. On Saturday afternoon the doctor came to my house and said that something was not right. He told me to meet him at the hospital on Sunday morning. I reminded him that the Lobo football team was playing its first game of the season at home and asked if he would let me go to the game. He said, "Absolutely not," but after some discussion, he agreed to let me go on the condition I meet him on Sunday morning at the hospital. That night we went to the game with me holding my side because of the pain, but at least we were at the game. I stood up for the kickoff and then sat down. I heard a swooshing sound, and the pain went away, but my leg began to tingle. I told Sally, "I am not sure what happened, but I do not think it is good." We felt it best to go to the hospital

Chapter 7: Father's Inspiration

right then. When we got there, the doctor in the emergency room called my doctor away from the game. I asked what it could be. He answered that it was probably the same as a ruptured appendix. My doctor arrived and rolled me into the operating room again. He told me that during the original operation he had seen a little infection, but he was not concerned. During that second emergency operation, he removed at least of a cup of staph infection. That was the reason for the pain. I now had more infection and things looked bad. I could die. He put me into the intensive care unit, and he tried several medicines, but they did not work. He told Sally that there was a new, powerful antibiotic, and he would try that. If it did not work, there was nothing else he could do to save me. Apparently, the new medicine worked, and in about two weeks I was able to return home. The whole church had been praying for me.

The other more positive event occurred after Hermosa was about two years old. I realized that there was a growing part of Albuquerque with no Baptist church. I went to our Associational Missionary and said that our church wanted to start a mission in that area. He responded that we were too small and that only a bigger church could start a mission. I then went to all the bigger churches in Albuquerque, telling them we would help them start a mission. They all had reasons why they could not do anything at that time. I went back to the missionary and said we were going to start a mission in the Northeast Heights area of Albuquerque. He called a meeting of the executive committee of the Association. We were invited to attend but had to sit in another room as they discussed our request. After about an hour, they called me in and told me that they were still opposed to a small church starting a mission, but they would not stand in the way and would give us their blessings.

I went back to Hermosa and asked if any of our members would be willing to go to that area and start a new mission. We only had about 120 members and six deacons. Half of the members and half of the deacons said they were ready to go. The church approved of them going. I drove out in the area and could not find anywhere to meet except for a small nursery school. I asked if we could use their building on Sundays for services. They told me that they could not make that decision; I needed to talk with Truett Sheriff, the owner of the building. I recognized the name. He was the head of all student work for the Baptists in New Mexico. He agreed to let us use his building.

I noticed that all the land around the nursery school was vacant, so I went to the city to see who owned it. I found out it was owned by two brothers, Calvin, and H. B. Horn. Both were deacons at the First Baptist Church. I met with them to ask if they would sell us some land. They said to come back in a week. When I went back, they said they would not sell us the land; rather they would give us four acres if we would promise to build a nice church building on the land. I agreed. I then went to a bank and said, "If we have land worth about $300,000, will you give us a loan for the same amount." They agreed. Thus, we had a place to meet, land on which to build, money for construction, sixty members, and three deacons to start the church. A captain in the air force who was also an ordained minister agreed to be the first pastor. We started Eastern Hills Baptist Church, what is now a strong church in that part of Albuquerque. A footnote is that Hermosa Drive lost one half of its members and one half of its deacons to the new church plant, yet within two months of their leaving, both the members and the deacons had been replaced with new members coming to the church. God had truly blessed that small church.

The beginning of Bill's First church in Albuquerque

A Completed Family

Candice was a beautiful child and the joy of our life, but now God blessed us again, this time with a healthy son we called William Mark. We were a little bit concerned since we were now making plans to go to a foreign country to serve and both children were still quite young, but our Lord assured us that He would take care of them. He has been true to His promise.

Now we were ready to enter another important phase of our lives—the fulfillment of the call to missions in Central Europe. We had been successful in planting two churches, and I had passed my test to get my engineering license. The biggest problem we still faced was that my father and Sally's mother were not excited about our plans. Also, the members of our church tried to talk us out of leaving, but we were convinced that going was God's will, particularly because everything had gone so well. Both of us were very certain that God had called us to be foreign missionaries, and it was important that we answer the call. Now it was time for the next step in our service to our Lord, but it was not an easy step.

Chapter 8

Faithful "Mitarbeiters"

> "The father buys, the son builds, the grandchild sells, and his son begs."
> **– An Old Scottish Proverb**

An Enduring Legacy

David McAlvany writes, "The history of the world is the story of great financial, cultural, and ethical legacies built in one generation, only to be squandered by second and third generations . . ." Another proverb states, "You can tell how successful parents have been by looking at their grandchildren." It is at this point that the realization comes that what has been accomplished could only happen with capable help from others. I have chosen a German word, *Mitarbeiter,* to use instead of a more common English word because in German the idea is much clearer. A translation of *Mitarbeiter* is a "with-worker." By far the greatest blessing that I have had is the love, support, and with-working from my immediate family. At every step of the way I have had support from a loving wife, obedient children, and capable grandchildren. All have been very faithful in their love for Jesus Christ and all have been committed to help in the mission of making Christ known to the nations. I would like to explain a little more about how important my immediate family has been to my success.

A Loving Wife

While I was a star on the Highland High School football team, I made friends with Connie Abbot, a cheerleader from our crosstown foes, the Albuquerque High School Bulldogs. We beat them for the first time at the big Thanksgiving football game in the fall of my senior year. Because of this defeat by the underdogs, the relationship between the schools was at rock bottom. Girls from AHS did not date boys from Highland. The next summer I began at the University. At registration, I met my friend Connie, and she was with another cheerleader from the same school. The other girl was extremely cute and had a terrific personality. I took notice, but she was from AHS. Also, at this time I already had a girlfriend and did not take a second look. Only months later, after I had broken up with my girlfriend, did I meet Sally Crook again. At that time, I was struggling with faith and had just made my decision to accept Jesus as Lord and Savior of my life. I was impressed with Sally; her sterling reputation and her beauty mixed with her great faith was impressive. We began to date and later she was an important influence in my decision to walk with Christ.

Sally was and is a special person. Not only was she beautiful but also very smart and had both feet on the ground. Some of the Albuquerque High football players who were my college teammates said that she was the only girl from their school who graduated as a virgin. I doubt that she was the only one, but their comment showed what her school mates thought of her. In a statewide contest by the Elks Club, she placed second as the most outstanding high school girl in the state. Such were her qualities. We both felt it was God's will that we marry and later that we go together as missionaries. That calling led us to Salzburg, Austria.

Missionary work is never easy. Even though we lived in the most beautiful city in the world, we did have some difficulties that came from living in Salzburg. We arrived in Austria about the time the movie *Sound of Music* came out, and I think that every Southern Baptist (sixteen million of them) wanted to visit Salzburg, and of course they wanted to visit their SBC missionaries. At the telephone office at the train station, our name was underlined and circled in the telephone book. In fact, so many visited that it became a real burden. We had an expression, *Menschen muede*, which meant that we were tired of people. One week we had so many visitors that on Saturday night we decided to stay home, turn out the lights so that no one would know we were home, not answer the telephone, but just sit alone in the dark. Sally had to bear the burden of entertaining so many people. She did a splendid job at this, but it was taxing.

In every decision that was made, Sally was equally important. We did not make decisions unilaterally but always together. We tried to stay in one place if possible so that we could put down roots. This worked to a degree, but being missionaries meant that we needed to move on some occasions. Sally was always up to making the move.

Two ministry areas in which Sally were teaching Masterlife and conducting "Color me Beautiful" classes. Masterlife was the discipleship course that we led with much success in our part of the world. Sally was one of the group leaders and helped put the many workshops together. When we were in Europe, using colors to determine how a person should dress became extremely popular. Sally took a "Color me Beautiful" course while on furlough and often ran programs for the women in the churches to determine which colors each lady looked best in. Her program was a big hit, and many in the church and youth groups loved her for her work.

Possibly the greatest contribution she made was just being a mother. Sally had graduated for the University with a degree in education and had worked for two years as a high school teacher, helping financially while I continued my ministerial studies. Being a teacher in another culture was not a possibility, so the Mission Board allowed her to have a job that was defined as "Home and Church." This designation gave her the opportunity to be a mother to the children as well as to help at the church. Being available at home for the children paid great dividends since she was always available to the children when she was needed.

Wagner Family

Sweet Candy

Sally had wanted to wait to have children until we had finished our education. It was probably just an accident, but the day our first child was expected was the exact day I graduated from Southwestern Baptist Theological Seminary with my Master of Divinity degree. Sally wanted to have the baby in Albuquerque since she had already moved there. I stayed in Ft. Worth for graduation. Luckily, the baby was two weeks late, so I could be in Albuquerque with Sally. I remember well the day of the birth. I was finished with school and thought I knew a lot, so I assumed I was ready for this event. Being calm and cool, I took Sally to the hospital when the time was right, and I stayed in the visitor's lounge. We arrived early in the afternoon, and at first, I had it all together. I was sure everything was going to be good, but with time I began to be more aware that many things can go wrong with the birth of a child. I eventually became a nervous wreck. I did not think this would happen to me, but it did. Late that evening the doctor come out to where I was. He was holding a bundle. The first thing I noticed was that he had slippers over his shoes and there was a lot of blood on them. My first though was that there had been problems. Not knowing anything about a birth, I suspected the worst. The doctor then handed me the bundle and said, "Mr. Wagner, here is your daughter." There she was. My whole life changed. I now had a completely different world view. This was my daughter!!! Later I found out that Sally was okay and that the delivery had gone as planned. Sally had always liked the name Candice and I liked the name Colleen, so we named her Candice Colleen Wagner. Sally did not want her to have the nickname of "Candy" but early in her life the name stuck. Only when she got married did we see a real problem with her name. She married a Texan named Scott Hoenig, whose last name means 'honey" in German, thus in Austria her name was 'Candy Honey." She has always been sweet. From an early age she was active in our youth work and while in school invited her friends to come to the youth center and to the church. She was the best missionary in the family and today there are many in Austria who owe their belief in Jesus Christ to Candy Honey.

An important decision on the part of all missionaries is where the kids will go to school. One reason we were sent to Salzburg was because there was an American school nearby in Berchtesgaden, Germany. They thought that the kids could go to school in English there. We believed, however, that the children should become a real part of the culture, so we made the decision to send the children to the Austrian schools. This decision both a good one and a bad one. The Austrian schools at that time were not very advanced in educational methodology, and the teachers often believed the best way to challenge children was to ridicule them. This practice did not work well with either Candy or Sally, but we tolerated it. Candy did well in both the elementary and secondary schools. Her educational process was not without problems, due partially to the different culture, but the Lord was gracious and gave us help when we needed it. By the time she was in her 40s, Sally had a pretty, gray streak in her solid black hair. She claimed it was because of the Austrian schools. Candice's last year of school was while we were on furlough, so she graduated from Sandia High School in Albuquerque and went on to Baylor University. The Mission Board always helps the children of the missionaries get their university education, something for which we were profoundly grateful. Candy got her degree in German and Education. Later she achieved her master's degree in Sports, Recreation, and Health. She became a high school German teacher and an excellent track and cross-country coach. She and her husband Scott are active in their local church in Mansfield, Texas.

Smart Mark

Our son was also born in Albuquerque, but before he was a year old, we moved to Austria. Candy could already talk when we arrive in Salzburg, but then she needed to learn German, while Mark grew up with both languages. When he was beginning to learn how to speak, he would stutter. It was so bad that we took him to an Austrian speech specialist. He asked if he was learning to speak both languages at the same time, and we said yes. The good doctor said not to worry; this problem happened often with children is these situations. Soon he stopped stuttering. Mark also went to the Austrian schools, but by this time we knew what to expect and he had fewer challenges as a student.

In bringing up the children, we decided to use the "love them but give them freedom" philosophy. It seemed to work. We told the kids that if they ever wanted to smoke a cigarette, they should come to us first, so one day Mark, followed by all his little friends, came to us and said he wanted to smoke. I went to the store and purchased a pack of cigarettes. Mark and all of his friends were waiting. I took Mark and sat him up on the kitchen counter, stuck a cigarette in his mouth, and lit it. He inhaled and started to cough. That was the last time he ever smoked. All his friends were amazed that he could come to his parents in order to smoke. Both kids had a close relationship to us.

Being an athlete in my younger years, I wanted the same for Mark. In the Austrian schools they did not have athletic programs, but the private clubs did. I wanted Mark to play soccer, so I enrolled him in a club when he was six years old. He still felt a little uneasy around the Austrians, so he asked if he could play goalie; that way he could be alone. The coach agreed. Later I tried to get him to go out in the field since he was the fastest boy on the team and later it was discovered that he was a good long jumper. He wanted to stay in the goal. With time he became an exceptionally good goalie. When he was fifteen, the coach for the sixteen and under Austrian National Team approached him about being their goalie. We were all excited, but two weeks later the coach withdrew the invitation. We wondered why until we were told that only citizens of Austria could be on the Austrian National team. When he made the invitation, the coach thought that" Markus Wagner," who spoke fluent Austrian dialect, was an Austrian. He continued to play soccer and run track in Austria.

The national sport in Austria is skiing. Because we worked with young people, we held two or three ski retreats a year for the youth. Both Candy and Mark became avid and capable skiers. Both children felt that it was important to do well in school as well as to keep up their physical health. These sports helped them to relate to others in Salzburg and allowed them both to use their talents in missionary work with other youth.

Other European missionaries had developed a system for educating their children. They would send them to English speaking school where possible, and if they did have to send them to the national school, it would only be for the early years. By the time they were in high school, they would either return to the U.S. or go to a boarding school. From about 1950 to 1980, only one missionary kid from the many Southern Baptists kids in Europe graduated from a European gymnasium. One reason was the system. Europe divided the kids in the eighth grade, and only the better students could go on to the gymnasium. Few could make this transition. In the case of Candy, she attended the gymnasium but did not need to finish the Austrian system because of the timing of our furlough. Mark, however, went through the system and was only the second MK to succeed in finishing with a degree. He then faced the decision to either go to a European university, which he could do, or return to the States for his university studies. He chose to return and attended Baylor University, completing a degree in German and History. From there he attended Southwestern Baptist Theological Seminary for both his master's and PhD. Today Mark and his family are Southern Baptist missionaries in Germany where he wears many hats, including teaching students in universities, seminaries, and Bible schools. He is also the chairman of the PhD. program at Olivet University and has written several books.

The Core Family

I am convinced that the most important part of a person's life is the relationships within the core family. When the family is happy together, then they can overcome many obstacles. From the very beginning of our family life, we decided that love would be the guiding part of our lives. Because God is love, this was an easy decision to make since God plays such an important part of everything that we do. Our children were taught to love each other even when there were childish spats. This attitude has carried over to adulthood. Today there are no arguments within the core family. God has blessed us in this area of life.

When the children were growing up, we took great care not to argue with each other in front of the children or to speak badly about others. We did not talk openly about other missionaries or problems in the church. When Mark was in the U.S. as a high school student, he came home one day and told us that there were some problems in the church he was attending. He did not know that churches had problems because we had protected him from seeing them in his early years. Church conflict was a new concept to him.

As the children were growing up, we made the decision to have Monday nights as time for the family, so we avoided all other meetings and contacts. As we observed this family night, each person was assigned a task: prepare a devotion, chose the songs, lead the prayer, and or chose a game to play. The responsibilities rotated so each got to do all four. Later we realized that both Candy and Mark had gained a certain expertise in public speaking and preaching because of the devotions. I must admit that the parents were not always happy with the games and songs the children chose, but it was a growing experience for all.

A Blessed Extended Family

The influence of my mother on the whole family was enormous. Both of my sisters, Dodie and Letty became strong Christians. Dodie was really the spiritual leader of the family after mother died and Letty started several ministries for the deaf in Albuquerque. I remember once that she won a rather large young deaf man to the Lord. His name was D.J. Once I came home on furlough and asked about D.J. and was told that the large eth moving machine he was driving rolled over on him and he died. But at the funeral all knew that he was in heaven because Letty had won him to the Lord. Letty was unusual in that she was 100% deaf in both ears and towards the last of her life he was also legally blind. This did not slow her down much. Every day she would take her three mile walk from home alone without any help. One day a car pulled out from their garage and ran over her and killed her. She too is in heaven with her Jesus.

Most of my nephews and nieces accepted Christ and now are serving the Lord. And now even their children also believe. The extended family was blessed by the history of the family going back many generations but mostly because of the faith of "Grandma Opal".

Another part of the extended family that has been blessed are my grandchildren. The children of Candice – Sophia, and Mathew and those of Mark – Kate and Natalie. All four are either in the university or finished. Sophia and Kate will go into counseling or social work while Matthew and Natalie are more into the area of technology. All four are healthy, beautiful young people. Again, all four have a deep and abiding love for Jesus Christ that was passed down to them by their parents.

Chapter 9

Foreign Missions

> "The hills are alive with the sound of music,
> With songs they have sung for a thousand years.
> The hills fill my heat with the sound of music,
> My heart wants to sing every song it hears."
> – Richard Rogers – Oscar Hammerstein II

Seeking Appointment

Any person desiring to be appointed as a missionary with the Foreign Mission Board had to go through an exceedingly difficult screening. Several requirements had to be met before a person could be appointed.

1. Recommendation from a church
2. An autobiographical paper in a length equal to one page for each year of
3. life for both husband and wife
4. Thirty different recommendations for each adult
5. Extensive medical clearance
6. Two days of psychiatric evaluation
7. A statement of beliefs
8. Numerous interviews with personnel associates
9. A seminary degree
10. A minimum of two years' experience in a pastorate.

In the four years after I had graduated from seminary, I had finished all the requirements. Then it was time to take the final step. Go!!!!

In the process of appointment, once candidates had finished all the requirements, an FMB associate would then recommend them to the appropriate committee for final approval. This approval occurred at the monthly meeting of the trustees of the Board. Dr. Keith Parks, our personnel associate, was a very capable man who later became the Executive Secretary of the Board. Keith assured us that we met all the requirements. In fact, we had even had many meetings with Dr. J. D. Hughey, one of my professors from Switzerland who was now the secretary for Europe. He too was positive about our being appointed, and he even stated that he wanted us to be the first Southern Baptist missionaries to the beautiful country of Austria.

The board meeting was to take place on a Tuesday. We were told that our names would be presented by Dr. Jesse Fletcher, the head of the personnel department. Dr. Fletcher would then call us with the results as soon as the final decision was made. At that time, I was working at the Laboratory. While I was at work the phone rang, and my secretary said that I had a long-distance call from Richmond, Virginia. I eagerly answered the phone. The dialogue went something like this:

> "Hello Bill, this is Jesse Fletcher. We just finished our meeting."
> I answered, "Well, Jesse was it a good meeting?"
> Jesse replied, "Yes it was a great meeting."
> I responded, "Did the Board discuss Sally and myself?"
> Jesse replied, "Yes, they sure did."
> I answered, "What was the result?"
> Jesse replied, "They turned you down; have a nice day – goodbye."

And then he hung up. I stood with the phone in my hand in complete shock. I could not believe what I had heard. We were not going to be appointed as missionaries. I thought that this must be some sort of joke. The phone discussion the next day was with Dr. Hughey. He confirmed the decision and said not to worry because he had another candidate who could take my place for Austria. Again, I was in shock. What possibly could have gone wrong?

Dr. Hughey then gave me an explanation. We were rejected by the psychiatrist. Everything else was in order, but they felt they needed to take the recommendation from the psychiatrist. Dr. Hughey explained that the psychiatrist had made two observations. The first was that Sally's mother was strongly against our going and that Sally and her mother had a strong bond. The second reason was that every time we left Albuquerque, I later wanted to return to the city and work in the Laboratory. The psychologist said that if we did go to Austria, we would stay only six months before resigning and returning home. Dr. Hughey then said there was nothing he could do. I asked if there was any way we could appeal the decision. He first said no, and then after hesitating he said that maybe there was a way. The Baptist World Alliance was going to meet in Florida later in the month and the Board's committees were going to meet again. If we would pay our travel and expenses to Florida, maybe we could make an appeal before the committee. We were ready to go.

Chapter 9: Foreign Missions

The committee did meet, and they gave us some time to explain our situation. Sally said that her relationship with her mother was strong but now she agreed to let her go. She stated that her commitment to missions was so strong that we would stay in our assigned post for our complete term. I told the committee that the reason I always returned to Albuquerque was because that was my home and I could make better money working at the Lab than I could anywhere else. At that meeting the committee changed their decision and recommended that we be appointed.

Encountering One More Problem

It was difficult going through this period of rejection by the Board. Many members of our family and the church were using the argument that this was God's way to say that we should stay in Albuquerque. For us to go to the mission field, it was necessary for us to attend a week's orientation in Richmond. If we did not attend, then we could not go. We were to fly out on a Friday for this important meeting. The Board had purchased tickets and we were ready, but the few days before we were to leave were filled with pressures and doubts. Should we go or stay? The longer we looked at all that had happened, the more doubts we had. Maybe we should stay. Early Friday morning Sally and I drove around the city praying and crying. What should we do? Finally, about four hours before the plane was to leave, we had made our decision. We would stay and not go as missionaries. We visited my mom and dad to tell them the news. They were concerned because they knew us well and knew all the problems. We told them that we were not going to the orientation and thus not going as missionaries.

My dad, the one who had wanted an engineer in the family, then asked me what would happen if we went to the orientation and then decided not to serve as foreign missionaries. My reply was that we would have to pay the Board back the money for the plane tickets and for the orientation. We did not have the money. Dad then said that we needed to get on the plane and go, and if we decided not to go to Europe, he would give me the money to pay the Board back. The last person I thought would help in such a situation was the one who was used by God to seal our going. Dr. T. B. Matson knew what he was talking about.

Moving to the Land of the Sound of Music

Salzburg, Austria, the setting for the movie *The Sound of Music,* is where we had been asked to serve. Doubtless, it is one of the most picturesque cities in the world, and the movie could not even truly show the beauty of the place.

On arriving in Europe, we met with Lewis Krause, our supervisor, and Isam and Katy Ballenger, who were going to serve in Germany. For several days, all three couples had a great time in Germany, and then Lewis drove us down to Salzburg. He showed us our temporary living quarters in a small hotel in the city. He told us there was a Baptist church with which we would work and that he heard there was a language school in the city. He also said that if we needed anything to give him a call. He then said goodbye and left. We were left alone to function on our own. This really was not a problem for us since we work well alone. Soon Brother August Hirnbock, the pastor of the church, came and visited us. He could not speak English, and we could not yet speak German, but we still had great fellowship.

Our first task was to learn the German language. We tried every school and method possible and eventually could function in German. Candice was only four years old, and Mark was barely one year old. The whole family got down to work learning to communicate in the language of the people around us. My job was to represent the Southern Baptist Convention to the Austrian Baptist Missions committee, which was a group of Baptists from different countries who was dedicated to helping the very weak Baptist Union of Austria. I was to go to two meetings a year and be active in the local church. Because we were learning the language, that was about all we could do. We did create the Austrian Baptist Mission of the FMB and remarked that we had only two members—Sally and me. Our business meetings were always very enjoyable with little conflict.

Beginning Our work with the Austrian Baptist Church

The church was rather small with only about one hundred attending. They met in a building that had been constructed in the 1930s. Brother Hirnbock was a very heavyset man who was loved and respected by all. The church had only a small youth group. Since we did not speak German, one of my first jobs was to form an English-speaking group that would meet on Sunday mornings after the German service. At that time there was no English-speaking church in Salzburg. This city of music is the home of the famous Mozarteum, a world-renowned music school for advanced students who want to perfect their talents. Many of these top musicians in the school were from other countries, and many had gained their first experiences in music in the church. Thus, from the beginning

Chapter 9: Foreign Missions

we had a good number of talented musicians. We often had very high-quality music performances sponsored by our English-speaking church.

After six months in temporary housing, we rented a house, so we started a German speaking Bible study. I still do not know how I did it, but I would teach in German. They still laugh about my many mistakes, but the work went well. One way the SBC was able to help in Austria was by giving the churches money to build new buildings. Salzburg was in line for one, and I led in the process of getting a new building in a city that did not appreciate the church being there. Because the city wanted to build a new football stadium next to the church and needed some of its property, they allowed us to tear down the old building and build a new one. That was when my engineering skills came in handy. I took the lead in designing the building and doing much of the foot work with the city. The building still stands as a useful place for worship.

The members of the church were extremely friendly, and we made many strong and lasting friendships with all. Even though the Austrian Baptist Union was small (650 members), they had good relationships. Much of this has to do with the great leadership of the Rabenau family from Vienna.

Bill With leaders of the Foreign Mission Board

Starting the Youth Center

Because my duties for the first two years only called for me to learn the language and go to two meetings a year, I decided to take over the small youth group (eight members) at the Salzburg church. In our churchwork prior to going to Austria, both Sally and I had been involved in youth and student ministries; therefore, it was natural that we would continue to make this a major emphasis in our work in Europe. With time we were able to bring in other youth who had previously not been active in the church.

After being in Austria for a year, we decided to investigate the possibility of having a student center for university students. Our director gave us the permission to rent a building for a coffee house to reach students. After several false starts we finally found a great little building in the center of the city. It was located at Berggasse 11. We rented the building and took the few kids in the youth group at the church and began a work. At this time, we did not have any university students in the church, but we did have some students who were in gymnasiums, which was the equivalent of an advanced high school; thus, we changed our first emphasis from university students to gymnasium students. Our young people worked hard in fixing up the place. It had previously been a slot car racing venue for youth. Now we needed to turn it into a coffee bar with a small auditorium for services. The day we began the renovations one young man came in looking for the slot car track. He asked what we were doing, and we told him that we were going to have a Christian youth center. Would he like to help? Indeed, he came back in the afternoon. Gunther Reinthaler became our first convert at the center and was one of our mainstays through many years. The Salzburg Baptist Youth Center was born.

We held evangelistic worship services every Saturday night. At first we had only a small group, but with time we attracted more and more young people until the room and the center were full. Many young people made decisions to accept Christ and to work with us. The center was run by the *Mitarbeiterkreis*. This word in German means that the young people themselves ran the center and made all the decisions. Allowing them this opportunity was successful. At one time the head of youth work for the city contacted me to ask why so many young people came to our center while the city also had centers, but no one came. I told her that we gave the young people something that no one else was giving them. She asked if we allowed dancing, alcohol, drugs, or smoking. The answer was no. "Why then do they come?" she asked. We explained, "Because we give them a living belief in Jesus Christ as their Savior." She could not believe that young people were interested in religion; what was interesting is that her own little sister was one of our leaders.

The Baptist Youth Center in Salzburg

A small problem was that we had a very high profile in the city. Everyone knew about us. The building had large plate glass windows that faced the street, and we put up a large sign on the upper windows that said, "Baptist Youth Center." The issue was that the Protestants had been hidden since the last of the nineteenth century. The Empress of Austria had at one time allowed the Lutherans to build their church buildings in the country, but the front door could not be on the main street. The Protestants did not like to be up front, and now here was the youth center being so visible. We never did solve the problem. Also, we tried to get the many young people to come to our church, but the church did not want as many as we were sending. In fact, the pastor asked me specifically not to bring more young people into the church. We had too many. At that point we began to send them to the Methodists, the Lutherans, and the Roman Catholics. We estimated that during the life of the youth center, more than 200 young people accepted Christ. Some of those who worked in the center went on to become full time servants for the Lord. Among those who either accepted Christ in the center or were co-workers are Henie Wagner, who is now a top Catholic priest in Salzburg, Emmanuel Wieser, the pastor of the Baptist church in Munich, Herwig Mauschitz, a pastor in the German Union, Tom Preston, one of the top

Lutheran pastors in Salzburg, and Walter Muller, founder and pastor of Visa del Sol, now the largest Baptist church in El Paso, Texas. Many from the center became lay leaders in churches in Germany, Italy, and Austria. There were so many capable youths that it is impossible to name them all. We were also blessed with a series of genuinely great journeymen. Among them were Perry Basset, Ron Henderson, Drexel Rayford, Jerry Jones, Charles Reynolds, and Eddie and Betty Alley. Other missionaries were always jealous that we always got the best journeymen. This was true, but a part of their success was the youth center and the great young people with whom they were privileged to work.

Doing Evangelism with University Students

Our original plan was to reach out to students at the University of Salzburg and the Mozarteum, but in the beginning we had too few students to do a solid work. With time some of our high school students graduated to the university, and we began to reach more of them. At first it was difficult to work with Austrian university students. They were all very smart, and all had taken many years of religious instruction in school, but they were not open to the Gospel as we presented it to them. They would come to our services and then go upstairs and have coffee with us and talk about religion. Generally, the talks were about some well-known liberal theologian, but a simple discussion about a belief in Jesus Christ was not feasible. My question was "How can we reach Austrian university students for Christ."

In attempting to find a solution I remembered an experience I had back when I was the pastor of Hermosa Drive Baptist Church. A friend of Sally's called me one day and said that she was being visited by a Jehovah's Witness (JW). She wanted Sally and me to be a part of the next discussion. We agreed, and on the given night Sally and I visited the home. We had a good discussion with Sally's friend and the young Jehovah's Witness. Because I had studied theology for many years, I had the answers, so I won the night. The lady of the house thanked us for coming, and we felt good.

About two weeks later the lady called again and asked us if we could come for another meeting. We agreed. This time we entered the house and the two ladies were again present, but this time there was an old Jehovah Witness lady in the corner, and she was ready for me. We argued for several hours without anyone giving in to the other. It is not possible to carry on a sensible conversation with a committed Jehovah's Witness. Each person speaks past the other. I finally suggested that we stop and pray to the living God and ask for his leadership in our discussion because we all wanted to find the truth. The older JW refused to pray. She claimed that I had a different God and that only her God was the true God. I replied that as we prayed, she could pray to her God and I would pray to my God, but we would pray. Again, she refused. I simply said, "Good, you can do what you want, but I am going to pray," and I fell on my knees and began to pray that God would be with us. The older JW lady picked up her books and left. JWs will not pray with evangelicals. I had won the night, not because of my knowledge of theology but rather because we brought the discussion into God's presence.

Youth at Salzburg Youth Center being led by Walter Mueller and Herwig Mauschitz

In working with university students, I remembered this experience, and I developed a method that worked very well with the students. After I got to know a student, I asked if he or she would be willing to devote fifteen minutes to an experiment that might help him or her know God. Because all students like experiments, almost all would agree. I then would tell them that we would go into our prayer room and both of us would get down on our knees and talk with God. I would pray first, and then I wanted them to pray. At this juncture about fifty percent would refuse. They knew they were no longer in their academic ballpark. Those who did pray often had a life changing experience with God.

I would pray first and ask God to work in the life of the student. Then it was the student's turn. Often, the young person would hesitate and then pray and then cry. The student was in the presence of God, and God saved them. Many students came to know Jesus Christ as savior by this method. It was simply allowing them to not only think intellectually about God but also to experience God.

Founding the Bible School

Because there was no evangelical Bible School in Austria, it was necessary for us to send students who desired to study further out of the country, generally to Germany. I questioned why we did not have a Bible School for evangelicals in Austria, and I was told the number of believers was too small to warrant one. After much prayer and discussion with our *Mitarbeiterkreis* in the youth center, we decided to start a Bible school in Salzburg. We took the idea to the Austrian Baptist Union, and they were cold towards the idea for three reasons: they did not want a school; they were against it being in Salzburg because those from Vienna felt that it should be in their city; and some leaders did not like the idea of their youths becoming full-time pastors.

The president of the Union was the son of a Baptist pastor, and their family had suffered much; thus, he did not think that young people should become pastors or even study in a Bible School. He was in the minority in this issue. Finally, the Union gave their permissions to start a school in Salzburg. We rented a nice building close to the city. By that time, we had several other missionaries who were working with us in Salzburg. Tom and Joyce Cleary, John and Jo Ann Hopper, and Allison and Sue Banks all became involved in the school. The highest number of students we had at one time in the school was twenty-five. They all lived in the school and attended classes there. They became active in our youth work.

We soon began to have some serious problems. Many young people from the Vienna churches wanted to attend the Bible School for one or two years, but the leadership of the largest church was against them going to Salzburg. It finally hit the critical point at a meeting of the Austrian Baptist Union. Those from Vienna controlled the Union, and they recommended that we close the school. Others wanted it to stay open. A vote was taken, and the results supported the closing of the school. I remember well that the wife of the leader stood up and said, "Do you mean to tell me that we gave Bill Wagner permission to open this school and now we are closing it. This is not a Christian thing to do." Her husband replied, "True, it might not be Christian, but it is the Austrian thing to do." The school was closed, and we continued to send our students to Germany.

Skiing and Schloss Mittersill

The most important sport in Austria is skiing. While we were in Albuquerque, both Sally and I did some skiing in New Mexico, but in Austria we took it up it big time. One of the main activities of the youth center was our ski weeks, when we would spend a week in the mountains doing both sports and Bible study. From the beginning of our time in Austria, I suggested that we buy a castle to be used for our youth work. We tried to buy several castles, but when the owners discovered that it was the Baptists who wanted to buy them, they always came up with an excuse not to sell to us. High in the Alps, however, was Schloss Mittersill, a beautiful castle overlooking a small Alpine village. I found out it might be available, but then I discovered that C. Stacy Woods, the leader of the Intervarsity student movement, had already made the arrangements to take it over. I told him of our desires, and he suggested that we work with him and use Mittersill for our needs. It was an ideal plan, and we then held many of our ski weeks there. In fact, the owners of Mittersill later wanted us, an Austrian entity, to take it over, and offered it to us for $20,000. The European Baptist Federation approved the sale, but the Austrian Baptists felt it was too large of a venture for the small Union and they put their veto on the deal.

Schloss Mittersill

Baptizing a young person in Salzburg

The Innsbruck Experience

For most of my first ten years in Austria, I also served as the Home Missions Secretary for the Union. I had a dream about how we as Baptists could have more influence in the county. I identified seven of the larger cities in the country and discovered that if a circle 200 kilometers in diameter was drawn on a map around each of the seven major cities, 95 percent of the population of the country would fall within these circles. We already had churches in four of the cities; thus, we needed to start churches in the other three. Then the larger churches would be responsible for starting missions within their circle. The Austrian Union did not like the idea since we had some small churches and they did not want to start new churches until these smaller churches were financially self-sufficient and had a full-time pastor. The problem was that these small churches would never be able to make it on their own, so we had a stand-off. The union would not approve of any new church starts. I tried many ways to get new work started until finally I gave them an ultimatum. Either they let me start a new church or we would leave Austria. They liked us and our family and did not want us to leave, so they gave us the needed permission. The three towns that needed churches were Bregenz in the West, Klagenfurt in the South, and Innsbruck in Tirol. Sally and I chose Innsbruck for a church plant.

Chapter 9: Foreign Missions

One of the motivating factors was our students in Salzburg. Many of them wanted to study in another university outside of Salzburg since the University of Salzburg was quite small. Most of them would study in Vienna or in Innsbruck. Vienna was best for those who loved music, and Innsbruck was good for those who loved sports. Our people were in the second category; thus, Innsbruck was their destination. Since eight youth from the youth center were studying in Innsbruck, I spent a year going down once a week to hold a Bible study. Then when we had permission to start a church, Sally and I moved our family to Innsbruck. The church began as a Bible study in our home. Because we had great kids from the Salzburg youth center, we began to grow rapidly. Soon our house was too small, and six months after starting in our home, everyone in the church began a search for a rented facility. Finally, one of our students found an ideal facility on the second floor of a building that was close to the center of the university. The problem was the rental price. It was high, and we wanted to do this without any outside help. One night, at the Bible study, we shared the problem and gave them the rental price. We then told them that we would pass around small pieces of paper and each one had to write down his or her name and the amount he or she could give each month towards the rental of the building. If we had enough money pledged, we would rent it; if not we would keep looking. When we gathered up the papers and counted how much had been pledged, we discovered that it was almost the exact amount needed with the equivalent of $1.50 over. We were not sure why God gave the extra $1.50. We rented the building, and it helped our work as we continued to grow.

Our leaders mostly came from our youth work in Salzburg, but few had any experience in running a church. That was where I could help. I told them that if someone wanted to be a member, they had to do four things. First, they needed to have Jesus Christ as their Savior. Second, they needed to promise to come to the main services when possible. Third, they needed to have a job in the church. Finally, they needed to contribute financially to the church. The job aspect was important since we wanted this to be their church. Some sang in the choir, some preached, some were greeters, and some were janitors. One outstanding medical student with an extremely high IQ had cleaning the toilets as his responsibility. The finances were also a question. They would ask how much they should give, and I would tell them to give a minimum of one Austrian Schilling or 4 cents a month. They would ask if that was all. I would confirm the amount. Then they would ask what the Bible teaches they should give. My reply was that they should give a tenth of their income. The students took this directive to heart. About six months after we started, the Austrian Baptist Union leadership made a study of how much each member of each church gave financially to the church. They calculated the average amount given by each member. In making the report they said that the amounts varied greatly because some churches had many businessmen and others were not so fortunate. When they gave the results, the church in Innsbruck gave twice as much per member as any of the other churches in Austria. Truly the students took their responsibility to God very seriously.

After a year and a half, the church had 64 members and about 100 in attendance every week. Of the 64, most of them were students in the university, and 34 of those were medical students. The students were all under pressure since the university had a reputation of flunking out students, especially those in the medical college. Often, we would pray long for students who had a test because if they failed it, they were out. I am happy to say that all 34 of the medical students now have their degrees and are practicing doctors. It was time for Sally and me to turn the church over to an Austrian as we were due to return to the U.S. for a year of furlough. Peter Torsky was a close disciple from Linz, Austria. I called him to come to Innsbruck to work with me and then take over the leadership. He and his wife Alita were great musicians and very dedicated. Peter did a fine job in taking over the church. Later, the church had to move to another location, but they continued to grow under Peter's leadership.

Wagner Family at a retreat in Mittersill

Chapter 9: Foreign Missions

When our furlough came to an end, we returned to Europe and visited Innsbruck. It should be noted that Austria is a strong Roman Catholic country and our young people had many problems being associated with the Baptists. We were considered a sect at the best and a cult at the worst. When our young people became Christians, they would tell their friends and parents. Their decision could be accepted since the Catholics were also considered Christians. The problem came when they were baptized. We never told the youth they must be baptized. We only said that they should study the Bible and see what it says about baptism. They all came to the same conclusion: they should be baptized. It was, however, always a decision that took courage. One young medical student from Tirol came to me and said that her parents told her that if she was baptized by us, she could no longer come home. We prayed and I let her make the decision. She wanted to be obedient to the Lord. She was baptized and for two months she was not welcomed home. After that she was again accepted by the family, and the parents became good friends of our church. Many of the young people had similar experiences, mainly because we drew mostly from well-to-do Austrian families. These were the ones who the Lord had led us to.

When we visited Innsbruck after our furlough, Peter said that they had four students who wanted to be baptized. Since I had always done the baptisms, he asked if I could I help him this time; I would baptize two and he would baptize two. I agreed. I had always had the baptism services in a river or lake early in the morning or some time when few people were around. This strategy had worked fine. I asked Peter when the baptism was going to take place, and he said the next Sunday after the church service, about 1:00 p.m. I asked where it would take place, and he gave me the name of the most popular swimming lake close to Innsbruck. It was July, so the weather was warm, and the lake would be crowded. I asked if we could change the time or the place since there would be many people, and he said no because others were going to meet us there. That Saturday night I prayed for rain. The next day was warm and beautiful, and after the sermon Peter told the church to follow me to our destination. We all got into cars and went up to the lake. In my car was Wolfgang, one of the four who were to be baptized. He was one of the brightest medical students in the school and a very capable young man. I asked him if his parents knew that he was going to be baptized, and he said yes. I asked if they agreed, and he said, "Not totally, but they are going to meet us up at the lake." This was an understatement

When we arrived at the lake, the parking lot was totally full. Finally, we were able to park all our cars a long way away and march to the lake itself. The whole church was following me. When we got to the lake, Wolfgang said, "Here come my father and mother." The father was a known politician in his city and the mother was a socialite. I had never met them. I remember well the mother's first words to me. In a loud voice she said," You are an evil man. You have ruined my son's future. You are a false teacher." Many people at the lake heard her and looked to see what was happening. I told Peter to talk with the parents since he had met them, and I took Wolfgang to the side. I said to him," Wolfgang, we have a serious problem. Your mother is not happy. Maybe we should put off your baptism until later and I can have some time with your parents." Wolfgang replied, "Brother Wagner, it was not you who called me to be baptized but rather Jesus Christ. I will be baptized." I agreed. By that time, the parents were more reasonable, and I told all the church to follow me. We finally found a place with only a few bathers. One after the other, the four young people stood and gave their testimony. We then proceeded with the baptism. I baptized Wolfgang, and as he came up out of, the water, he raised his hands and said, "Praise the Lord." Afterwards the parents said they were greatly impressed with what they saw. God had given us another solution to a difficult situation.

Today the Innsbruck Baptist Church is a strong living church with many of the earlier students still being the leaders. Others from that group have moved to various German speaking cities and have taken over leadership positions in churches. Peter Torsky is now the pastor of the Baptist church in Bad Ischl, Austria.

Innsbruck was a blessing to our whole family. We are often asked, "How well did your children do in a foreign country." Both Candice and Mark are remarkable young people. Often missionary kids will go to international schools since the national schools are so different. Both of our kids went to the Austrian schools and did well. I remember one time in Innsbruck when Mark was a new arrival in the class. The teacher asked if all in the class were from Innsbruck. Mark said no. Then the teacher asked if all the kids were from Tirol. Again, Mark said no. She then said she assumed that all of them were Austrian—again his answer was no. Finally, she said that surely all of them were Roman Catholics. Mark again said no; he was a Baptist. He was ready to stand up for who he was. One year later he was elected the president of the class.

CHAPTER 10

Freedom in the Spirit

"All of them were filled with the Holy Spirit and began to speak in other tongues as the Spirit enabled them."
Acts 2:4

The Answer to Success

During the active yeas of the ministry of the Salzburg Youth Center, a teacher from a German Bible school visited us to learn the reason for our success. At the beginning of our discussion, he stated that we were lucky to be in Austria where it was easy to minister because in Germany it was awfully hard to get something like a youth center off the ground. This was the first time anyone had ever stated to me that Austria was open for our type of ministry. The two countries in Western Europe that had the reputation of being the most difficult were Austria and Belgium, the two countries where I lived for most of my time in Europe. Both countries experienced revivals with the common people during the reformation times but both converted back to Catholicism during the counterreformation. Some give this as reason for the lack of many Protestant and evangelical churches.

Now I needed to respond to the visitor from Germany. My answer was quite simple. We relied upon the power of the Holy Spirit, and He seemed to just carry us. I am aware that many will use the Spirit as an excuse for what bad is happening and for what good is happening, but l honestly believe that we experienced a tremendous outpouring of the Holy Spirit during our time at the youth center.

In trying to understand why the Spirit choose to bless us, we needed to remember that the youth center operated during the time of the Jesus Movement that brought young people from all the world to Christ. This movement began in California and spread to many other countries. I feel that we were just the representatives of the movement in Austria.

The Charismatic Influence

It is impossible to speak about the Holy Spirit working in churches without considering both the charismatic and the Pentecostal influences. I visited many expressions of the Jesus Movement in many countries, and there seemed to always be the divide between those who taught the baptism of the Holy Spirit together with speaking in tongues and those who did not. Which was correct was generally an active question. Our work at the youth center fell into the second group, or those who did not emphasis the tongue gifts. Many who visited our services were convinced that the lively services proved that we were charismatics, but we remained evangelical in our theology and activities.

When we moved to Innsbruck, our reputation followed us, and I was visited by a young Roman Catholic priest who had come to Innsbruck to teach about the charismatic movement in the Catholic church. He had been a part of the charismatic awakening at Notre Dame and now was going to do missionary work at the University of Innsbruck. He had been given my name as one who would be sympathetic to his message. We did have many hours of good fellowship, and I did help him in many ways, but he kept trying to get me to speak in tongues, saying that I needed the baptism of the Holy Spirit. He did admit, however, that he felt I had the Holy Spirit but without the tongues.

A New Spiritual Experience

During our time of revival at Salzburg, many told me that I could have an even a greater ministry if I only experienced the baptism of the Holy Spirit. Of course, my desire was to be used by Jesus in the greatest way possible; thus, I needed to consider what I was being told. Often, I would pray that if the Lord wanted me to have that baptism or speak in tongues, He should work in my life in a way that I would have that experience.

One night about the midpoint in our revival, I had a rather unusual spiritual experience. I decided to spend several hours in prayer in my living room late at night when I was alone. My request to the Lord was that if He wanted me to have this so-called Pentecostal experience, I was open to whatever God wanted for me. After several hours of prayer, I began to speak in a language that I did not understand. I assumed that it was what other say was biblical speaking in tongues. This went on for about three minutes. Then I abruptly stopped and the Lord spoke to me and told me that He had given me this brief experience to show me that He could give me the gift of speaking in tongues if He so desired but that this was not to

Chapter 10: Freedom in the Spirit

be one of my spiritual gifts. I never spoke in tongues again after that night. Also, during this experience, God told me that my gift would be that when I spoke in German, the Spirit would be with me and give me the words to say. After this experience I marveled that even though I had a difficult time learning another language because of my dyslexia, God would help me in preaching and speaking German. I even had a German teacher who once remarked, "Mr. Wagner, I cannot understand how you can speak such good fluent German, but your writing of German is atrocious." I felt that the power of God went with me, and I would much rather speak German so that people could understand me than in an unknown tongue. I do not argue against the concept of speaking in tongues, but I believe that it is a gift given to some but not to all.

Many of my Pentecostal collogues told me that I needed to speak in tongues, and then I would relate this experience to them. They often replied that God does not work that way. My reply was that I kept telling God that, but He told me He was happy with me as I was. We continued to work with young people, being fully conscience that the Holy Spirit was guiding us in almost all we did.

Ministering in the Holy Spirit

Without the tongues or the prevalent theology of the baptism of the Holy Spirit, we continued to minister, being fully aware that the Holy Spirit was leading us. How was it possible that the Spirit was so present in what we were doing? In looking back, I see that we attempted to do the same five things Nehemiah did when he heard that the walls of Jerusalem had been destroyed

First, he sat down. We were continually active in what we did at the center, but we also spent much time seeking the will of the Father. We did not try new methods or try to follow what other had done but rather we sat in the present of our Lord and allowed Him to show us what we needed to do. Watchman Nee, the Chinese theologian, wrote a book called *Sit, Walk, Stand* in which he said the first action a person should take in the start of a new life or a new work is to sit and listen to the Lord. This we tried to do.

Second, he cried. I have always been amazed that often when the Lord is working in the life of a person there are tears. Many times, in our prayer meetings when we saw the lostness of the Austrian young people, our tears flowed. Many times, in our prayer room after we had been on our knees, attempting to explain to a student how to become a Christian, there were tears when the person did accept Christ. I never knew why, but it seemed that when we were in the presence of the great creator God, there were tears.

Third, Nehemiah mourned. Mourning and crying are two different activities. Crying is limited in time and intensity while mourning is continuous. Often, I would walk either alone or with some of my young people through the streets of Salzburg and pray for those we would pass. Not knowing who they were, we still asked God to show us their spiritual condition, and often He did so. This knowledge would then lead to spiritual mourning. We were compelled do all we could to bring them the Gospel. This desire led us to hold many street services in the center of Salzburg, one of the world's greatest tourist attractions. During these times, some young people would come and join us; thus, we continued to grow.

One day when we were preaching on the street, one of my coworkers bought an Asian young man to me. He did not speak German so my friend thought I could speak with him in English. I asked if he could speak English, He replied:" No, Chinese, Chinese", I then asked him if he could speak German, he Replied "No, I Chinese, Chinese. I was not sure what to do then so I handed him Christian tract in German, and he said, "Ah so" and he reached into his pocket and handed me a Christian tract in Chinese. I said "Jesus" and he smiled and replied "Jesus, Jesus". I then remembered that the one word that is the same in all the languages in the world is "Hallelujah". I spoke this word and he replied with Hallelujah. We repeated this word many times. We could not understand one another but we were still communicating that Jesus was Lord. We had many great experiences holding services on the streets of Salzburg.

Fourth, Nehemiah fasted. I realize that fasting is not a common activity in some churches, but our young people felt this practice was a necessary task. Often when we would go on a retreat away from the city, we would fast for the entire time, generally three days. I did not need to try to get them to fast; they all felt this was a part of their faith. Often individuals in the group would practice individual fasting to come closer to God.

The last of Nehemiah's five activities was prayer. For all our youth, prayer was a central activity. We had a prayer room in the center, and it was used both before and after every service. Many young people came to faith in this room of prayer. An important activity was our all-night meetings that we held about every six months. Because our home was the best place to meet, about thirty youth would join us there and pray all night. After these meetings, we would always receive a special blessing from the Lord. Prayer made a difference.

Reaching all Youth

As I stated earlier, we were active during the time of the Jesus Revolution, so other churches in Austria and Germany were also working with youth. One other active youth program was at the church in Gratz with their pastor Graham Lange. Graham was a deeply spiritual English man who desired to win as many to the Lord as possible. His situation was somewhat different from ours. Graham saw the large number of hippy type youth who would sit in the center of the city with their bongo drums and guitars. He went to these young people and invited them to come to his church, which he changed into a youth center. He had some success and in a rather short period of time he had about thirty young people in his group. At that time, we had about fifty. His problem was that these youth were not willing to make any firm commitments; thus, they left his work soon after joining it. His work collapsed because he had few solid types who would remain in the faith.

Our approach was different. The Lord led us to have contact with students in several of the gymnasiums. We began with only about four gymnasium students, but then one by one others were won. Walter Mueller, one of our original members, took Christian books such as *The Cross and the Switchblade* to school and gave them to the students to read in a week. He then took the books back and gave them to another student. Several top students came to faith by this method. Of the students in the leadership circle, almost all came from solid Salzburg families and were more mature than most at that age. This did not mean that we avoided the street youths. No, we made a real effort to reach out to every young person, but we had an unwritten rule that for each problem youth with whom we worked, we needed to have three solid youth to help care for them. The problem youth could take all our time and energy, so we needed to find a balance between the need to help everyone and the time needed to do other work. This strategy seemed to work well.

Among the street people we reached was Herwig Mauschitz, who later became the pastor of a large Baptist church in Germany, Helmut Wrywoder, who later became the Billy Graham Film Representative for Austria, and a youth named Hans. Hans was interesting. He was a wayward youth who took drugs and begged on the street, but he had a great spirit. He came to the center regularly, but he was always a problem person, and many of youth did all they could to help him. One night as we had finished a service, Hans came into the Center and said to me, "Bother Wagner, my mother who lived in Steyer just died, and I want to go to the funeral. Could you give me money for a train trip to Steyer?"

I replied, "Of course, we can go down to the train station together. I will buy a ticket and write on it "cannot be exchanged for cash." He then stated, "That's okay. I can hitchhike, but can you give me money to buy some flowers for the funeral?" Again, I said, "Certainly, we can go down to the flower shop at the train station and I will buy the flowers and tell them they cannot be exchanged for cash."

At that point Hans said, "Brother Wagner, do you see this fist? If you do not give me some money, I will knock you through this plate glass window." I replied, "Where do you want me to stand? Tell me and you can hit away." He then said "Brother Wagner, you are my best friend. I love you like a brother. Please give me some money." I said, "No," and he left. About five years after this encounter, I was on the streets of Salzburg and a nice-looking young man greeted me. I did not recognize him. It was Hans. He told me how the center and Jesus had helped him and now he had a job and was doing well.

We ministered to all types but always had many good strong committed Christian kids that acted as our base.

Working with other Christian Organizations:

I thought it was rather strange, when I was seeking appointment to be a Southern Baptist Missionary, that my personal advisor mentioned that it was a negative that I had so many contacts with other Christian organizations in the past. As a pastor at Hermosa Drive, I had contacts with Campus for Christ, Youth for Christ, Christian Businessmen, and others. I saw this as positive, but others thought it was not good that I had so many contacts outside of the Baptist World. While at the church I and another man, Connie Alexander, a sports newscaster, founder the New Mexico Chapter of the Fellowship of Christian Athletics. I was always interested in discovering how others were working for Christ.

After becoming a missionary, I kept my contacts open to these various organizations. In fact, in 1966 I was asked if I could arrange a place for a new organization that wanted to come to Europe to meet. I found a place close to Salzburg and met with them. I was told then that this was the first meeting of the Campus Crusade for Christ in Europe. Later, as the Youth Center was going well, I was contacted by Rev. Bob Broyles and Bill Starr of Young Life. They wanted me to help them get Young Life started in Europe. I helped them and later as the youth center closed, many of our young people continued to work with Young Life.

As a young missionary in 1965, I did not know many of the leaders of the Christian church in Europe, so when I learned that Billy Graham was

Chapter 10: Freedom in the Spirit

going to hold a worldwide Conference on Evangelization in Berlin, I wanted to attend but I did not have the necessary contacts. I wrote the director of the conference and asked if they needed anyone else from Austria. I received a reply that said yes, they only had two from Austria and I could be the third. I attended the World Conference on Evangelism in Berlin in 1966 conference and all the following conferences that later formed the Lausanne Movement. One person mentioned that I was one of the very few that had attended all the Lausanne major conferences that have been held since its beginning. An outgrowth of this was that I became the contact person in Austria for the Billy Graham Organization.

After arriving in Austria, one of my dreams was to buy a castle and develop a youth ministry from the castle. While I was looking, I was told that C. Stacey Woods of Intervarsity had just obtained a beautiful castle in the Alps called Mittersill. As already mentioned, we worked closely with Woods on the development of the castle. This let us to have a close relationship with InterVarsity and with their program in Austria, called the Austrian Student Mission. We gave a lot of help to them especially in Salzburg and Vienna.

CHAPTER 11

Further Studies

"We who know the gospel have been given the greatest gift in all the world ... Therefore, we cannot – we must not – stay silent with this gospel."
– David Platt

Studying in Austria

While we were living in Salzburg I wanted to make as many contacts with the student community as possible; thus, I made the decision to enroll at the University of Salzburg. My purpose was to make contacts and to study theology from a Catholic perspective. Since the University was sponsored by the Roman Catholic Bishop of Salzburg, I would be taught from that view. I did not really understand the European educational system, but when I went to the registration office, they informed me that I first needed to get permission from Dr. Schmidt, the head of the theology department. I made an appointment with the esteemed doctor. Upon entering his office my first words to him were "Dr. Schmidt, my name is Bill Wagner." His rebuttal came swiftly: "I am not Dr. Schmidt. I am University Professor Dr. Schmidt." Then I began to understand the strict division of positions in the European faculty system.

After correcting myself, I informed him that I was a graduate from a university, had a master's degree from a Baptist seminary, and wanted to study theology in his school. He quickly told me that they could accept only students who had studied Greek. I informed him that I had taken two years of Greek. He seemed surprised. He then told me that only those who knew Hebrew could study with them. Again, I informed him that I had two years of Hebrew. Upon hearing this, he allowed me to enroll in one course, which was Post Reformation Theology. I was ready. The catalog gave the time and place when the course would start. I was there on time, but no one else was present, including the professor. This occurred the first three times the class was to be held. I went the fourth time, and the room was full, and the professor was present. I asked another student why no one had come the first three times, and I was informed that this professor always missed the first three sessions. It was apparent that the professor was king. When the professor began his lecture, he taught in Latin. "Latin!!! I thought, I do not know Latin." I returned to Dr. Schmidt to tell him of my problem. He could not believe that anyone who has studied Greek and Hebrew had not studied Latin. It was truly a Roman Catholic university. I then transferred into the History Department, which taught in German. I studied for a year at the University of Salzburg.

Experiencing Burn Out!

My first ten years at my work were very enjoyable, but later I began to take on more than I could handle. The growth of the youth center coupled with the building of the church, my work as Home Mission Secretary, and the demands of being pastor of the English church took its toll. After ten years, the FMB wanted to make several movies on mission work, and the leaders of the Board recommended that our work in the Youth Center should be the basis of one of the movies. The producer and director came to interview me, but it was at a low time in my burnout. After the interview, they agreed to look elsewhere for a good example. I was finished. When a person really has burnout, it is difficult to function. He or she may keep doing what is needed but without any real joy or energy. At the end of the ten years I was burned out.

Our family was due a furlough, which both Sally and I truly needed. The question came as to where we would go and what we would do. I thought about doing graduate work. Once before I had applied for a Doctor of Ministry program at an SBC Seminary, but I was turned down because of my low grades. I thought I would try again. Many recommended that I begin work on a Doctor of Missiology degree. A PhD was out of the question. At one time while I was in college, we thought about Golden Gate Baptist Theological Seminary but decided to attend Southwestern instead. Again, we felt that Golden Gate might be the best place to study since it was in the West. However, the school with the best reputation for missions was Fuller Seminary in California; it had an outstanding Doctor of Missiology program. I applied for both, and with time I was accepted by both. The time came when I needed to decide. Our director wanted us to go to an SBC seminary; thus, Golden Gate was the natural choice. One night I sat at my desk and studied the numerous letters I had received from both schools. Those from Golden Gate were formal, and they kept saying that maybe I could be accepted. Finally, I received a formal letter from Fuller with a statement of my acceptance. The letters from Dr. Art Glasser, the Dean of the School of World Missions, were very encouraging. They said that only two from Europe had done their Doctor of Missiology degree with them and they were excited to have me work with them. They wanted to learn more about Europe from me. They really wanted me to attend Fuller. The decision was made. I attended The School of World Missions at Fuller in Pasadena, California. Later I was told that when Dr. Hughey requested the funds to help me in my studies he requested help for me to study at Fuller Seminary, but later he crossed out Fuller and just said Seminary. It was taboo to go outside of the convention.

With Billy Graham and Otto Diebelius in Berlin for World Conference on Evangelism, Berlin 1966

Going to Fuller

One problem many students encounter at the doctoral level is the languages. I was told that I needed German or French as well as Greek and Hebrew. By that time, I was fluent in German, so I did not even have to take a test, and they gave me credit for my other two languages, even with my bad grades. Now I could study missions. The D. Miss program was a minimum of three years with the last year being a dissertation.

They looked over my history and were able to give me some credit for the year at UNM before we went Rüschlikon and for my time at the University of Salzburg. I spent a full year in Pasadena and took some courses in the summer and then wrote the dissertation, which took several years. Finally, in 1975, I graduated with a Doctor of Missiology degree. I was asked to give the student response at graduation.

During the last year in which I was writing my dissertation, Fuller Seminary received approval from their accrediting agency to offer a Ph.D. in Missions. This was considered a step higher than my D. Miss degree. When it was made known that Fuller now could offer this degree, my mentor, Dr. Art Glasser, asked the theology faculty if four worthy students from the School of World Missions could transfer their work over to the Ph.D. program. His argument was that the four of us were excellent students and that we qualified for entrance into the Ph.D. Program. The professors in the School of Theology turned down the request. We would have to start over in the PhD. program. Dr. Glasser was not happy with this decision. Dr. David Bosch, a good friend of his, was the Dean of the School of Theology at the University of South Africa. Dr. Bosch was one of the top missiologists in the world and a renowned scholar. He asked Dr. Bosch if the four of us could use our D. Miss degree as a steppingstone into his Th.D. program. Dr. Bosch agreed and gave us credit for our work at Fuller. I did need to do about a year's extra work first but was then allowed to write my Th.D. dissertation. After many years in the program I received my Th.D. degree form UNISA.

Reading and Writing

From the first grade on reading had been a problem for me. Even after earning several degrees and having years of valuable experience, I still had dyslexia. Now in graduate school where I was forced to read a great number of books, the problem was more extreme. I continued to use my speed-reading technique. I was a great visual learner and so used pictures and video when possible. Once I was given an I.Q. test and was told that I scored 130 on it, which was a surprise to my teacher. Intelligence was not the problem; dyslexia was.

Once I entered the Doctor of Missiology program, I had to write a dissertation, which was the equivalent of a book. I found that I liked writing; it was reading that gave me a problem. I also was blessed with the ability to retain what I had learned so that I could use the material in my writing. Also organizing my thoughts came easily. In writing a dissertation one needs to do a great deal of research. When I was in junior high school, we had to write a composite theme. All the students had to do research in books and put down the ideas or quotes on 3x5 cards. All the other students dreaded the composite theme, but I enjoyed doing it. I liked this type of writing, so I would go to a book or magazine and pick out what I needed and put it on a card and use it. I found this method worked in my post graduate work just as it had in junior high. Later, when I wrote longer papers or even my books, I realized that I had no ability to proof read what I had written and correct the spelling and grammar; thus I worked up a system where I would find someone who had talent in this area. I have no problem with calling on those more gifted than I am in an area to help.

At Fuller, where I wrote my first dissertation, they were interested in Church Growth. I had been told that a student needs to write on a subject about which he or she knows more about than the professor does, so I wrote on the growth and decline of the German Baptist Union. In this work I needed to do much research on statistics and comparisons. This was an area where I excelled because of my engineering background. In fact, while I was at Fuller, Dr. Ralph Winters came to me and said that he noticed that I had an engineering degree. I said yes. He then told me that four of the six professors in the School of World Missions had engineering degrees, including himself. He said that engineers make the best church growth people because they think more practically.

I used the same method for research and writing at the University of South Africa, and it worked. My second book, a study of American Missionaries working in Europe, was again on a subject that I knew well.

Publishing My First Books

My first dissertation was entitled *New Move Forward in Europe* with the subtitle of *A Study in the Growth and Decline of the German Speaking Baptists in Europe*. This theme was also a great help to me since I did a lot of study of the Austrian Baptist Union. My dissertation was published in a book and sold well since it was only the second major church growth study of a European group. I was proud of my first book, and when it was published my mother said she wanted to read it. I gave her a copy. After she finished, I asked her how she liked it. She replied, "Well, it wasn't one of those books you can't put down." She was not interested in the science of church growth.

My second dissertation, *American Protestant Missionaries Working in Western Europe* was also published and well received. Neither of the books could possibly be best sellers, but those in the study of missions were pleased with what I had written.

Serving as Consultant for Evangelism and Church Growth

Very soon after I received my D. Miss degree from Fuller, the Foreign Mission Board announced that they were changing their structure and were dividing the world into four basic regions. In each region they would appoint a Consultant for Evangelism and Church Growth. Mainly because of my degree and my book on German speaking Europe, I was chosen to be the consultant for our region. Areas such as Latin America or Africa were somewhat homogeneous, but Europe was too small to stand alone, as was the Middle East; thus, they put the two areas together and my region was called Europe, North Africa, and the Middle East. My responsibilities covered both East and West Europe and the Islamic countries. It was a large area, but I discovered it was an exciting area at that time. Western Europe was Secular, Eastern Europe Communist, and the Middle East and North Africa were Muslim except for Israel, which was Jewish. I had much to learn about this region.

Discovering Masterlife

At this stage of my life, I began to ask a simple but significant question: "How can we (the IMB and I) as a foreign entity help the churches the most in my region." Dr. Avery Willis, a fellow missionary, invited me to a discipleship workshop featuring Masterlife, a program that he had developed. Little did I know that discipleship would become the major emphasis of my life for the next ten years.

Earlier I had heard the story about a young fisherman who owned a small boat. He was out on the Mediterranean Sea one morning when a large yacht sent out a distress signal that it was sinking. The young man sailed to the larger boat and rescued the owner of the yacht. The owner was very wealthy and wanted to give the young man a large reward for his good deed. The young sailor refused, saying he had done nothing special. The wealthy man insisted. At that point, the younger man asked the man to give him one cent on the first day of March and to double it every day until the end of the month. The man stated that he was very wealthy and could give him more if he wanted. The young man wanted only what he had requested. The request was agreed to and on March 1, the young man received one cent. The next day it was two cents and the next day four. On the eighth day the accumulative amount reached the first dollar.

The amount that the boy received at the end of the time was, however, over $20,000,000. The theory of multiplication was in effect rather that the theory of addition. The same is true for discipleship. Jesus Christ told his disciples that they must make disciples of all nations, an impossible task we might say, but it is very much attainable if we use multiplication.

I tell people that if I were to take a small group of them down to the heart of their city and preach and 3000 accepted the message and came to Christ, the same number that believed in the second chapter of Acts, we would consider this a great success. If we did it again the next day and then the next, we would rejoice. The only problem is that it would take us more than 2100 years to reach every man woman and child now alive for Christ. This is not the answer. However, if we went into the city and won two persons to the Lord and spent six months discipling them and then told them to do the same and they both did it and the process continued, it would take only seventeen and a half years to win every person. Discipleship is the Lord's way to carry out the Great Commission.

Sally helping at a MasterLife Workshop

The dynamics of Masterlife are simple. A potential teacher needs to come to a four-day workshop and learn about the course. He or she can then teach the course, which lasts for six months, with the suggested group of eight meeting together two hours a week every week but doing homework every day. When a person has finished the course, then that person can also lead a group of eight persons. It is not a complicated system. As I began to promote this method of discipleship, my hope was that I could reach first the leaders of the various Baptist Unions and sell them on the program and then hold workshops in all the countries of my region. In our first workshop, which was held in Germany, we had the leaders of nine Baptist Unions. At the end of the workshop every leader felt that the program could function well within their Baptist unions. We began to develop plans to both translate the materials into various languages and to hold workshops in those countries that were open to discipleship. At later workshops we invited other Baptist leaders who were not present at the first workshop to attend, and the process repeated itself. The plan worked as designed.

After a seven-year period was finished, the success was impressive. Masterlife had been translated into 19 of the languages in the region, 150 workshops had been held in 28 countries, and this discipleship course was being used in 32 countries of the region. We could confirm that over 24,000 had taken the course. We made a small study of some of the fastest growing churches in the region, and almost everyone used this course as an important ingredient of their growth. Masterlife is still used today in many of the countries, with Germany being the best example of how it has grown.

CHAPTER 12

Finding New Directions

"Ask, and it will be given to you, seek and you will find, knock and the door will be opened to you. For everyone who asks receives, he who seeks finds; and to him who knocks, the door will be opened."
– **Matthew 7:7-8**

In my new job as Regional Consultant, I discovered that I needed to have contacts with both national leaders and missionaries in all the countries of the region. MasterLife gave me a wonderful opportunity to do just that, but the new position also made it necessary for me to travel a great deal in the region. It was truly a vast region stretching from Portugal in the west to the tip of Siberia on the east, and to the Arctic Circle in Norway to Yemen in the south. In my region there were secular Europeans, communist Eastern Europeans, Muslim Middle Easterners, and Jews in Israel. My knowledge of the European regions was strong, but I had a learning curve when it came to North Africa and the Middle East.

My job description stated that I was to visit the mission meeting of the various IMB missions when strategy was a topic. I could help by giving advice. In most cases the missions did this work satisfactorily. One of my main contributions was in helping them know what had been done in the past. A good example took place in the Middle East and North Africa. The Area Secretary called together a high-level strategy planning meeting with mission leaders and National Union presidents. It was an expensive meeting that was held in Cyprus and lasted for a week. At the end, a good thoughtful strategy had been developed and it was given to each union. The problem was that it was not communicated as well as it should have been. Three years later I was present in one of the countries, and they had just appointed a committee to develop a strategy for their mission. All the members of the committee were new missionaries. As they started, they began at point zero. I asked about the work that had already been done, and they knew nothing about it. We then studied what had already been finished and built upon this good plan.

Working in the Middle East

Because I did not have experience in the Middle East, I was careful to listen well to the missionaries. We were operating a hospital in Yemen; it was the only truly Christian institution in the county at that time. Some others had been closed. Our people were somewhat afraid of having me there because they did not want open evangelism. The second time I visited the country, I arrived early on Sunday and went to a hotel in the capital city of Sana'a, about a five-hour drive from our hospital. Since I always run every day, I went to my room and put on my running clothes. As I began to run out of the hotel, I saw a dark-skinned young man on the street with a big black book under his arm. It looked like a Bible. I approached him and learned that he spoke English and that he was a Christian from the Philippines. He was on his way to the International Church meeting at the auditorium of an international oil company. When I asked where he lived, he pointed to a window in a building next to the hotel. It had a large wooden cross on it. He worked and lived in the hotel. We went to church and had a wonderful time. The church could not advertise, but it could operate. After I returned to the hotel, I entertained a steady stream of Christian young men who now knew about me, and they came to visit me.

Several years after my first experience with the International Church in Sana'a, we had an event at the hospital. Some extremists were trying to get the hospital shut down, and they had brought the issue to court. During the court session some young men appeared as witnesses and described one of our Christian services. They said that practically nude women danced wildly in front of the alter just as the pagans do. We could not begin to think about where they had gotten this. Only later did we discover that the large auditorium, located in the center of Sana'a, was owned by a western oil company, and was used for a variety of events. On Tuesday nights the international women held an aerobics class in it. Some of the young men had seen them and associated their exercises with the church.

Our work in Yemen is no longer open. It was always a dangerous place to work, and towards its end a terrorist came into the hospital and killed three of our missionaries, including a wonderful woman missionary doctor. One time while we were there, shots were fired in the streets and it appeared as if there was going to be a civil war between North and South Yemen. We left before too much happened.

Possibly the most unique country in my region was Morocco. We loved it there, probably because it has a desert climate like that of New

Chapter 12: Finding New Directions

Mexico. On one of our trips there I was asked to teach the leaders and the pastors how to function in a hostile society, so I drew on my experiences in Eastern Europe. They seemed to like my teachings on this subject. At the time I was staying with one of our missionaries in Tangiers. The seminar was held from Tuesday to Thursday. Late on Friday afternoon we learned that all Moroccan Christians in the country were being arrested and put in jail. Apparently, the authorities had been planning this for some time, and they even intercepted correspondence courses that were being sent in from Europe. Many were now in jail. I was with our missionary, and he discovered that a young couple who ran our bookstore in Fez had been arrested in Tangiers. They were both young, and the wife was about seven months pregnant. The missionary was concerned, so he went to the jail with food and bedding because in Moroccan jails neither was available to the prisoners. He tried to leave them for those in prison, but the jailer refused to allow it. The missionary returned home, and we held a whole night prayer vigil. We were especially praying for the young wife and her condition. About eleven in the evening there was a knock at the door. There stood the young woman. Wiping away her tears, she explained that she had walked about three miles to us. She related that when the missionary was at the jail, they could hear the conversation but were not allowed to speak. When he left, the jailer came and let the young woman leave, but kept the husband. She then walked to the missionary's home.

The next day I preached in the English-speaking church in the city, and later in the day Dr. Jimmy Draper, then the President of the Southern Baptist Convention, arrived Morocco for a visit. We met with Jimmy, who was an old friend of mine from high school days and told him of the problem. Together we went to the American Ambassador, who was a believing Christian, and he took us to the Home Secretary for the Government. We told him of the predicament and reminded him that Morocco was a signatory to the Human Rights Agreement of the United Nations and that guaranteed freedom of religion. His answer was classical. He said it was the Foreign Department that signed that statement and he represented the Home Department; thus, he had no part of this promise. He then said he would see what he could do, and later that day all the Christians were released.

In the same country we had a bookstore close to the university in the city of Fez where we sold textbooks along with Christian books and Bibles. One day the authorities came in and confiscated all the books. We were distressed because of the loss of good literature. Several months later I was in a luxury hotel in the capital of Morocco and went to their bookstore where I found many of our Christian books and Bibles on sale with the logo of our bookstore printed inside. The books were now being sold on the open market. Even though the closing of the bookstore saddened us, we then realized that we had much better distribution after the authorities confiscated the books.

During my time in the Middle East a civil war took place in Lebanon. We could not fly into the country but had to take a ship and port in the Christian section and then travel overland to our seminary, which was located on a mountain overlooking the city of Beirut. At night we would go up on the roof of one of the houses and look out over the city. We drank tea and watched each side shell the other in the valley. I asked if any shells every landed that far up and was told that close to us a tree had been hit, and the leader pointed to several craters where shells had hit. We then continued drinking tea. One day I went down to the center of the city where we had a high school run by Jim and Wynona Ragland. They were totally committed to staying to run the school. They had many harrowing experiences. When I visited them and spent the night, I was warned that during the night I would hear rockets going overhead. Those in the North were firing at those in the South and those in the South were retuning fire. He said not to worry since few landed where we were staying. It was not an enjoyable night. Sally went with me on one trip and at that time many Americans were being taken hostage. We were warned not to speak English and not to look too American. Sally was convinced that I had a loud voice, and she strongly encouraged me to stay quiet.

Once we decided to visit Damascus. Both Sally and Candice were with me, and we were told that we should visit the large mosque in the city, the Mosque of John the Baptist. Tradition was that the head of John was in the tomb in the middle of the mosque. We could visit it, but both ladies had to wear black burkas with veils. There were several other ladies with us, and when I looked at the group of them, I could not tell them apart. I walked separately from them. I have a habit to pray, sometimes loudly, when I am visiting a church or a mosque. As I was walking around, I was praying under my breath. My prayers were for the Muslims in Syria. In telling the story further, Sally says that because of my "loud" whispering, she thought I was singing, and soon I was surrounded by about fifteen brown shirted young Muslims. She was convinced that they were going to kill me for singing or preaching in their mosque. It is true that I was surrounded by the young men; however, all they did was ask why I was in the mosque. They were not concerned about my praying. I told them I was a simple tourist. When I asked who they were, and they said they were revolutionaries from Iran. We then had a discussion on the merits of our two religions and parted peacefully. Later I got the reputation in the Middle East as the missionary who was caught singing in the mosque. The story grew legs with time. An interesting sidelight to this story occurred about two years later when I was visiting with one of our missionary families in Jordan. After diner we all sat around the table and told missionary stories. At one point the twelve years old son of the missionary said "Daddy, tell them about the crazy missionary who was singing in the Mosque. The father being somewhat embarrassed said "Son that was Dr. Wagner".

Bill playing soccer with the youth in Jordan

Working in Eastern Europe

Kazakhstan

I loved my work in Eastern Europe. The Church was always under great pressure, but the Christians had a great faith and the fellowship with them was always warm and uplifting. One of my favorite areas was in Central Asia, in countries such as Kazakhstan and Kirghizstan. Both were introduced to Masterlife and used it well. I also helped by teaching in a new Bible school in Bishkek, the capital city of Kirghizstan. While traveling in Russia and Central Asia, I generally flew with Aeroflot, the national airline, but after the Berlin wall came down several new airlines came into existence, including Trans Aero, which used Boeing 727s.

I was once ticketed to fly from Alma Ata in Kazakhstan to Moscow on this new airline. We were supposed to leave at 8:00 a.m. but we were delayed, finally boarding the plane at 4:00 p.m. We were ready for takeoff with, as usual, passengers in every available seat, including the jump seat. Some of the passengers' packages were on the floor. I was sitting next to a Jewish reporter from a large New York newspaper; he was stationed in Alma Ata. The plane began to taxi for takeoff, and we had reached about 80 percent of the necessary take off speed when there was a loud explosion under where I was sitting. I knew at once that we had blown a tire, but I also knew that the 727 had two tires on each side and could land and take off on only one tire. The pilot also knew that, so after the plane shook for about a minute, he gained more speed and we were about ready to take off again. Suddenly, there was a second explosion in the same area. The second tire had also blown out. Now the plane began to shake and serve violently. I mentioned to the man sitting next to me that this was the end. The plane kept moving down the runway until the pilot was finally able to regain control and come to a stop. The pilot announced in stuttering English, "Will you please all exit the plane." When we got out, we noticed that the wheel casing and the wheels were completely gone on one side and the plane's wing on that side was only about two inches off the ground. There was also fire at that location, but it was extinguished quickly. That night the reporter invited me to stay with him, and I had a great time witnessing to him. I tried to contact my wife but could not, but the reporter contacted his girlfriend and told her to call Sally. Unfortunately, when she called Sally all she said was, "There was a plane crash and your husband was on it. Goodbye." Sally had no idea if I had been killed or not. The next day I contacted her to tell her that all was in order.

East Germany

Another interesting experience in Eastern Europe took place in Berlin. We were holding a Masterlife Workshop in the East German Baptist Seminary outside of East Berlin. As it was taking place, we noticed many large black autos stopping at the school. City officials were there to talk with the leader of the school. We knew that politically much was happening in the country, but we did not know the details. Before the workshop was finished, I asked one of my co-workers, who was the pastor of the Baptist Church in Rostock on the North Sea, how he was going to get home. He said by train. I asked how long that would take, and he said about seven hours since he had to change trains three times. I deter-

Chapter 12: Finding New Directions

mined that it would take only half of the time if he went by car, so I asked if I could drive him home. He agreed. After the workshop ended on Friday morning, we took off for the North. As we were arriving in Rostock, the pastor told me that every major city in East Germany had agreed to demonstrate against the government on a different night during the week. Friday was the day for Rostock. He asked if I wanted to join in. "Yes," I said.

The plan was that since there were four main churches in the city, everyone would meet in one of the four and at 8 p.m., all would come out and have a large demonstration and parade. As we were walking to the center of the city, we passed a large four-story building. I was told that this was the headquarters of the Stasi or the secret police. We could walk past the building but were not allowed to stop. We then arrived at one of the churches in the city, and when it was 8 p.m. we went out on the street. Someone stuck a sign in one of my hands and a candle in the other. We eventually arrived at the dark Stasi building and all the demonstrators chanted, *Stasi raus, macht daraus ein Krankenhaus:* "Secret police get out and make this building into a hospital." After the demonstration, we went to the pastor's home for a late supper.

As we were eating, he wanted to hear the evening news, and what was said on the radio was truly shocking. The announcer said that as of that time all East German citizens could leave the country without a visa. The pastor's son said the wall was down, and he got in a car and drove to Berlin. We all rejoiced, but I thought that now if everyone could leave East Germany, I would have a hard time getting out. There was one small border crossing up in the North not far away, so I made the decision to get up early in the morning and drive there to get out. As I was driving to the northern crossing, I said to myself, "Bill Wagner, this is one of the most important days in the history of your country, Germany. You are a fool to leave," so I turned around and went to East Berlin and on to the Brandenburg Gate where CNN, CBS and NBC were filming, and I remained the whole day as young people were climbing over the wall in both directions. I asked a policeman what he was doing, and he answered that he had no idea. He said, "I am just trying to see that no one gets hurt." Later that evening I drove to my crossing in the South, and it took me eight hours to get out. I spent the next day in the West German border town of Hof interviewing East Germans who were in the West for the first time. It was completely new to them. I took many of them to McDonald's for hamburgers. It was truly a great experience.

Russia

Another notable event in Eastern Europe took place after the Wall came down. I traveled to Moscow where there was going to be a meeting of Baptist leaders. At that time there was much chaos in Russia and the government was now in the hands of Boris Yeltsin. There were many in the country who wanted to return to the old system of communism, thus the unrest.

I arrived in Moscow two days early and was met by our missionary, Norman Lytle, and he told me that our plans had been changed and that I was supposed to stay in a medium-priced hotel on the outskirts of the city. I was the only one staying there that night. I arrived at the hotel early in the evening of the first day and checked in. I asked where I could eat and was told that all restaurants were closed because of a lack of food but that the big Cosmos Hotel about three miles away might be open, so I walked the distance and found it open. I ate and began my walk back to my hotel. On the way about 15 young men in black leather jackets came running towards me and one asked in English, "Where is the Hotel Cosmos." I pointed the way and they ran on. Several were carrying little red flags. As I continued walking back to my hotel, I heard what I thought were fireworks. The sound was rather loud and consistent. I also saw some rockets go up, but they did not explode in a beautiful burst; rather they just fell to the ground. I thought to myself, "Even the Russian fireworks are faulty."

Upon reaching the hotel I went in on the back side and up to my room on the fourth floor. As I started to go in, one of the ladies of the hotel had a key, rushed into my room, and closed the blinds and rushed out again, saying something in Russian. Also, there was a note on the door from Norman; it said, "Bill do not leave the hotel. Yeltsin has declared an emergency. "I still heard the fireworks as I went into my room and looked out of the window. There about 25 yards from the side of the hotel was a large building that I later discovered was the national headquarters of Russian television and around it was tanks and soldiers firing into the building. What I had thought were fireworks was live gunfire and what I had thought were simply fireworks in the air were rockets all round. As I watched, I was not sure what to do, so I just sat down and watched. After a few hours it all stopped. The next day I discovered that the communists had taken over the station and the government was trying to get it back. They succeeded. Because I run every day, I went out to run and went over to the building but was told by a tank commander to get away. I did as he requested; however, I picked up several small red flags. These were the ones I had seen being carried by the communist young men earlier. Then I decided to jog in another direction but did not see any other disturbances.

After I returned to the hotel, I had the whole day free, so I decided to take the subway into the center of the city. When I arrived, I asked what was happening and someone pointed me to the parliament building, so I walked towards it on one of the main avenues. From about three blocks away I could see that tanks firing into it. I came to a place where tanks and soldiers would not let any of us get closer. I stood with about a hundred other and watched. Then over the loudspeaker something was said in Russian and all the others turned and ran. I believe in 'When in Rome, do as the Romans do"; thus, I did the same. All around me people were falling. I thought they are shooting at us. This was not the case, but people were tripping over each other in their haste. I hid behind a large tree and later everyone started coming back. I stayed awhile and then returned to my hotel. Everything after that was somewhat normal. The mini revolution was over.

The Gift of Miracles

One of the spiritual gifts mentioned in II Corinthians 12 is either "miracles" or "miraculous powers," depending on the translation. Many times, I have taught on the spiritual gifts and during the lecture I will ask the participants to tell me which of the gifs they possess. I do not believe that even one time the gift of miracles was mentioned. The reason is not because God does not do miracles in our lives but rather because we are not ready to recognize the wonderful hand of God in doing what is unexpected. I believe that miracles are simply God doing what is both unexpected and unexplainable from nature's point of view. The pastor of Hoffman Town Baptist Church, Norman Boshoff, once asked me, "Bill, what are your spiritual gifts?" I then listed what I believed were the gifts that had been given to me by the Holy Spirit. One of those gifs was the "gift of miracles." He was pleased that I knew what my gifts were.

Some may think that anyone who can list his gifts is self-centered, but I believe every Christian who has been saved for over six months should have an idea of what his or her spiritual gifts are. Since the gifts are to be used to lift up the Church, it is impossible for us to do what God wants if we do not know what gifts God has given us. A miracle is not like turning the day into night but rather it is the power of God working in our lives to do what is not explainable. When a miracle does happen, the person involved should never be the one to receive the praise but rather the glory belongs to the Lord. Let me give four examples of how I think God has done the miraculous in my life.

Death and Dying

It is worth noting that three times I should have died, but in each case, God allowed me to live. These are miracles performed in my life by the creator God. Another interesting aspect in my life is that very few persons whom I know or who have been members of my church have died. I have been ordained for over sixty-two years and have pastored ten churches, but only three members of the churches I have pastored have died. One reason is that in most of the churches we worked in consisted mainly of young people, but there were also many older persons. We never had anyone die in an automobile accident or in a violent way. In my many years as a Christian I have attended fewer than twenty funerals and led in only nine of them. I have performed over fifty weddings, twenty-two ordinations, and hundreds of baptisms, but only nine funerals. I see this as a great blessing from God; in fact, I would see this even as a miracle.

London

After leaving the church in Innsbruck, we settled in Belgium. One of my great loves was holding revivals for churches, and I was often asked to lead in either a spiritual campaign or a church revival. On one occasion I was invited to preach a revival meeting at a Baptist church in London, England. The pastor had also been in contact with an American Baptist Church and they were going to send five lay people to help in the meetings. I saw this as a great opportunity to serve the Lord. The meetings were to start on the Sunday morning, but I arrived early on the Saturday before the meetings were to begin. My flight arrived before 8:00 a.m., and I went directly to my hotel, which was in Central London, next to the world-famous Hyde Park. When I checked in, the porter said I had a message from the pastor waiting for me. Bad news!! Of the five persons who were supposed to help, only two could come. This left us with a need for more help. In my room I prayed that God would send us somebody to help. After my prayer, I followed my usual morning routine of putting on my running clothes and going for a run in Hyde Park.

In the center of Hyde Park there is only one café, the Serpentine Café. It had tables outside, and on that day it was full. As I ran by the café, I thought I heard a voice cry out "Bill.," but I thought to myself that no one in London knew I was there, so I kept running. About 200 meters past the café, I thought I better go back since there might be someone who knew

Chapter 12: Finding New Directions

me. As I returned to the cafe, I saw Gerda sitting at one of the tables. She was a student from the Innsbruck Church, and I had baptized her. She asked me what I was doing in London, and I told about the coming revival meetings. When I asked her why she was there, she explained that she had a week's break from the university and had asked God in prayer what she should do with the time. God had told her to go to London. She had been obedient and taken a train to London, not knowing what she was going to do. After arriving in London, she looked in a telephone book for the nearest Baptist Church and discovered that it was closed but would open for the next service, which were on Sunday at 10:00 a.m. She then took her suitcase and went to the park, found the café, and sat down at the table and prayed, "God what shall I do now?" Then I ran by. Many will say this was just a strange coincidence, but for me, this was a miracle of God. Gerda helped us in the revival, taking the place of those who could not come. Three young people were convinced to become believers because of Gerda's influence.

Austria

While working as the Home Mission Secretary for the Baptists of Austria, we were searching for a piece of land on which to build a youth retreat center. At one point it appeared as if we had found the right piece of land. It was located by Albert Ortman, one of the deacons of the church. He made the arrangements for several of us to look at the land, which was about 50 miles from Salzburg. On the morning of the day we were to check it out, I was with Dr Gerhard Claas, the Executive Secretary of the German Baptist Union. The plan was for us to drive down in the morning and meet with Mr. Ortman at 2:00 p.m. at the property. Our problem was that we had been delayed. As we were traveling on the autobahn towards Salzburg, it became apparent we could not make it on time, and I needed to let Mr. Ortman know of the problem. We stopped at a service station on the Autobahn to make a call using a coin operated telephone. I had only one two-German Mark coin so I could make only one call. I did not know Mr. Ortman's number, but I did know that he lived right behind us in Salzburg, so I decided to call Sally and have her get the message to the Ortmans, either by phone or by going their home. The telephone had a rotary dial, and I dialed my home phone number. Apparently when I was dialing, I paused in the motion several times, but still someone answered the phone. I heard the usual Austrian way of answering the phone by giving their name: "Here Ortman." I recognized the voice as Elfriede Ortman, the wife of Albert. When I asked if Albert was there, she said no, so I asked if she could get the message to him. She agreed and hung up. I was baffled. I had called Sally, but Elfriede had answered the phone. "Yes," I thought, "I know what had happened. Elfriede was undoubtedly at our house and Sally had her answer the phone." The problem was solved.

When I arrived home, I asked Sally about this and she said Elfriede had not been at our house. I later discovered that their telephone number was almost the same as ours, with only one digit different. While dialing, I made a mistake and ended up calling the persons with whom I needed to talk. Again, maybe it was just a strange coincidence, but I see this as God doing miracles in the lives of those who serve Him.

India

There were four of us who were Evangelism Consultants for the whole world. On some occasions each would invite others to visit his area. I received an invitation to spend a month in India. I was not prepared to see the immense poverty in that country. It was hard to accept that I was helpless to do anything to relive their suffering. I remember a five-year-old little girl wrapping herself around my leg and crying that she was hungry. The missionaries said that I could not give her anything. I thought this was too harsh. Many children asked me for candy, so I went to a store and bought some candy to give out. I gave out about three pieces, and then I was inundated with kids. I do not know where they came from, but I could not get away. The missionary pulled me out of the crowd and said, "I told you not to give them anything."

During my visit to India, I was invited to preach a revival at Jambo, a small Christian community in Eastern India. It was hard to reach. We went first by car, then small boat, and later walked. Around a corner I came to the Baptist church in Jambo. That night I preached. At the end of the message one of the elders came to me and said that the Lord had told them that I had the gift of healing and that there was a lady in the church who was very sick. "Would I come and pray for her?" I agreed but under the conditions that the elders of the church would come with me and that we would anoint her with oil as we prayed. They agreed, and they took me into a small house. In the main room on a large stone slab lay a small older lady. I thought she had a fever, but I was not sure. I was certain, however, that she was extremely sick. We all laid hands on her, anointed her with oil, and prayed. The next day, as I came back to the church, I was told that she was healed, and they thanked me. They said that others in the church, including the pastor, were sick. They asked if I would I pray and lay hands on them also. I agreed, under the same conditions, so I went to all of them and many of them were healed. The pastor was suffering from malaria and he was healed. I was thrilled.

When the week was over, I could hardly wait until I got back to Europe. I would become a famous faith healer and have large healing crusades, but before I left for home, I became sick with stomach problems. At that time, I thought since I had healed those in Jambo, I could heal myself. It did not work. When I got home, I went to a doctor and he gave the correct medicine. Back in Belgium, I no longer had the gift of healing. I learned that God gives the gifts to whom He will and at the time that best suits Him.

It is impossible to say enough about my many experiences in Eastern Europe. Hungary, Romania, Moldavia, and other countries in the world. Many whom I met were so special. God was working in all these countries, and I made many warm and lasting friendships.

Bill preaching a revival in Indonesia

Chapter 13

Faculty Status

"Wherever God Leads, Follow.
Whatever God Promises, Believe.
Whenever God Tests, Trust.
However God Blesses, Share."
– **Charles Swindoll**

Becoming a Professor

While I was a student in seminary, many of my student friends expressed a desire to become professors in a university or a seminary, something that was never my goal or my desire. I just wanted to be either a preacher in a church or a missionary overseas. I think God must have a real sense of humor in that he allowed me to become a professor while many of my friends failed to reach that goal.

After I received my first doctoral degree, I began to be asked to teach in various Baptist seminaries. My father always said that it was far easier to teach in a university than in a grade school. Even though he was a professor and chairman of the department at the University of New Mexico, he was not allowed to teach a first-grade class in an elementary school because he did not have the appropriate teaching credentials. This was now true for me.

Upon our return to the mission field from doing my doctoral work for the Doctor of Missiology, I began my new career as a consultant. It was suggested that we move out of Austria since the situation was the same as the old pastor staying in a church when the new younger pastor needed to be the one to serve. New missionaries had been appointed to serve in Austria, so I was no longer needed there. We agreed to move from our beloved Austria, but the question was where? Sally and I made lists of our preferences of where we could live. Her top pick, Brussels, Belgium, happened to be my last choice. As one can imagine, we finally chose Brussels. My main concern was that those in Belgium did not speak German. I refused to learn another language, but Sally argued that it was truly an international city and was considered the capital of Europe. We found a lovely house in the French speaking section of the country in the small town of Ohain, which is located in the famous battlegrounds of Waterloo. We stayed there for ten years.

Prior to leaving for our stay at Fuller, I had held a Masterlife workshop in Schloss Mittersill, and Dr. Theo Kunst from Belgium brought all his students from his newly started seminary. They were all impressed with the course. A year later, when Dr. Kunst learned that we had just moved to Belgium, he visited me and asked if I would help him in the founding of his new seminary connected with the Belgium Bible Institute. I agreed.

Joining the Evangelical Theological Faculty

The Belgian Bible Institute is a well-respected Bible Institute that had been founded in the city of Brussels after the World War I by missionaries. It has two sections, a French speaking school, and a Flemish speaking school. They purchased a large Catholic Seminary building that had well over 500 rooms and a large section of land. It was in the cultural city of Leuven, about twenty miles east of Brussels. As soon as they had the facilities, the leadership wanted to start a full-fledged seminary. Dr. Theo Kunst from the Netherlands had just received his PhD. from Dallas Theological Seminary, so they asked him to start the school; the Evangelical Theological Faculty (ETF) was born. He was ideally suited for the task. The school had been going for about two years when he asked me to help him.

About the time I arrived a series of events occurred that were God inspired. One of the professors from the newly founded ETF was witnessing and contacted a young man from the Flemish section. After a period of time, the young man became a Christian. Soon he wanted to study at the seminary, but he too had problems with his father, who was against the idea. The father asked the son if this new seminary was accredited by the government of Belgium. The answer was negative. The father was a top politician in Belgium, and he said no son of his was going to go to an unaccredited school; thus, the father called his good friend, the Head of Education for the country. He asked his friend if there were theological seminaries in Belgium that were accredited, and he received the answer that there were two, a Catholic school in Leuven and a Protestant one at the University of Brussels. The father then asked if there was an Evangelical one, and the answer was no. They both agreed to investigate the possibility of accrediting the ETF.

One day Dr. Kunst was invited to go to the office of the head of the Department of Education and was told that because of the long history of the BBI and its good reputation, the department had agreed to give the new school full accreditation. Dr. Kunst reported that as they were preparing the official papers, the head of the Department of Education stated that they could now offer an accredited Licentiate Degree (Masters) in Theology. He then looked at Dr. Kunst and asked if he also wanted an accredited Ph.D. Degree; Dr. Kunst said yes. The school was now accredited to offer the equivalent of a master's in theology and a Ph.D. in Theology. This was a wonderful opportunity for the evangelicals in all of Europe.

When I agreed to work with the ETF, Dr. Kunst asked me if I had ever put together a PhD. program. I replied no but said that I was willing to try. I knew how the two programs that I had finished functioned and was ready to see what I could do. I was reminded that we had little budget and only three professors who possessed valid doctors' degrees. We did have a large building and a great administration as well as s splendid reputation in Belgium. It was a challenge.

The accreditation from the Belgium Government alone was worth its weight in gold. We had an official letter from the king of Belgium giving us that right. No other evangelical school on the continent of Europe even came close to having what we had. We knew we must be careful and create a valid program and that it was necessary to leverage what we had if we were going to be successful. I needed to work at first in three areas: the form of education, the faculty, and the students.

First, the form. The University of South Africa (UNISA) also had state recognition, and it offered a PhD. program that was basically a program of education by distance. The students were not residential while at that time in America all programs at that level were residential. At UNISA each student was assigned a mentor, and he or she would work closely with that mentor. The student would also take courses given by other professors, but still the main emphasis was a strong mentoring by one professor. Also, the students were expected to come on a regular basis to the main campus in Pretoria to visit and work with their professors. How often was determined based on several factors. I felt that we could use the same method as UNISA and we would assign each student a mentor, but unlike in South Africa, we would hold a yearly two-week colloquium where all the students and faculty members would come to our school to meet. At that time, the students and faculty would present academic papers that they had been working on. This way the faculty could observe the progress of the students. Each professor would develop the academic program for his or her student based on the student's previous work and experience. This plan was put into place, and it worked well. At first, we received some criticism from other universities, but with time most of the other universities adopted a similar plan.

The second problem was who would be the professors. In Europe, the title of "University Professor" was very prestigious. Only recognized universities could offer this title to their professors. Western Europe had several highly qualified evangelical teachers with recognized doctoral degrees who were not related to universities. We had men such as Dr. Peter Beyerhaus, who did carry the title of University Professor from Tubingen in Germany. I selected ten of those evangelicals with PhD degrees, asked if they would be willing to be on our adjunct faculty. We could not pay them a salary, but we could pay their expenses and we could officially offer them the title of "University Professor." Their responsibility would be to mentor up to three students, attend the yearly colloquium, and be a professor on our faculty. None refused, and thus we now had ten top European evangelical faculty members on our faculty. The next step was finding the students. Each student had to qualify for doctoral studies at the university of their own country. We were amazed as to the number of students who wanted to study with us. Early, we had twenty-five students from ten countries studying with our ten professors. The doctoral program was off and running.

After about four years there was an almost complete breakdown of the total school in Leuven. The government of Leuven would no longer allow the French speaking BBI to hold classes in the Flemish speaking part of Belgium, and they had to move. There were many personnel problems in the school, and one by one most of the administrators resigned, including Dr. Theo Kunst. At one time the master's program at the ETF had thirty students, but it was now down to ten. Only the doctoral program was growing. At that time, a professor from the Netherlands and I had to take full responsibility for the school.

One day, a committee from the school visited me at home and asked if I would consider being the president of the ETF. At the time, it seemed like a dream job for me. I agreed to investigate it. I then asked the FMB if they would second me to the ETF so that I could remain a missionary but work at the school. Because the school was not Baptist, they refused, but they did allow me to continue to work one fourth time in the school. To turn down this offer was exceedingly difficult for me, but it was the right thing to do. For several years I functioned as the president of the school without having the official designation and officially only working one forth time at the school. Later both the BBI and the ETF began to regain stability, and another person was asked to be the full-time president. I continued as the head of the doctoral program. Later the doctoral program was capped at forty students, and it now had eighteen professors. I then turned the leadership of the program over to Dr. Donald Tinder, one of our professors. I continued to be one of the doctoral professors for the first twenty-five years of the program, but once I reached the milestone of serving for a quarter of a century, I decided to retire. This was my first retirement.

With my work at the ETF, I now found myself being called professor. I had never had that as a goal; I just seemed to fall into that position because I wanted to help a friend in the creation of a new seminary. When he was young, my father seemed to have the same dilemma. He never wanted to be a professor, but he became one. He often said to the family, "When I was young, I could not spell professor; now I are one." I guess that my experiences also allowed me to say, "Now I are one."

Faculty and Students at a Colloquium for the Evangelical Theology Faculty Belgium

Starting the Bible Seminary in Bonn

A spin off the ETF was the founding of another seminary in Europe. One of the first students in the doctoral program at the ETF was a young German by the name of Heinrich Loewen. He came from a particular people group called the "Russian-German Immigrants." This people group came into existence between 1650 and 1930, when many Germans immigrated to Russia to find a better life. They put down their roots and lived in many parts of Russia but retained their German language and culture. They were scattered over the country. Most of them were somewhat prosperous since they were hard workers, and many were evangelical and Lutheran Christians. Because of these factors, they were greatly persecuted in Russia.

At the start of World War II, Stalin and Hitler signed a non-aggression pact that Hitler broke early in the war when he invaded the Soviet Union. After this event, Stalin was extremely upset and sent the Germans living in Russia to places such as Central Asia and Siberia. When the trains arrived, the refugees were pushed out to fend for themselves. Many did not survive. They often refer to this as the Christian holocaust. I was told many horror stories of what took place. This is a story that needs to be told. In the 1980s a treaty was signed between the USSR and Germany that allowed these German speaking citizens to return to Germany,

I was in the airport in the early 1980s, returning by air from Moscow to Frankfurt. I saw about 300 rather poor looking refugees sitting on their suitcases in a corner of the departure lounge. I asked who these people were and learned they were Russian-Germans and were awaiting the few seats available to fly to Germany.

They came in mass, and after a few years were integrated back into their mother county. Most of them were people of great ability and were also were hard workers. The evangelical Christians among them were encouraged to integrate into Baptist or similar churches. The problem was that those from the USSR were very conservative and did not really fit into the more moderate Baptist churches. One of the immigrants told me, "German Baptist leaders both smoke and drink beer." This was true. As the Russian Germans came to Germany, they began to create their own churches and even their own denominations alongside those already existing in Germany. In time they became a strong influence in the religious scene in Germany. A study of them revealed there were at least seven well defined groups of them, ranging from very fundamental to moderate. In fact, some of the largest numbers in attendance in German churches on a given Sunday were at these immigrant churches, sometime running over 5000 members.

In the late 1980s a group of these churches wanted to start a Bible seminary since they felt that the Baptist schools were too liberal. The main church behind this new start was in Bonn, and its pastor was a dynamic leader by the name of Victor Zierat. Victor had a vision of a Bible seminary, and he held a meeting in a hotel in central Germany to outline his plans. I was invited to attend this gathering. He drew a large circle and then added a small one in the middle of it. He then divided the circle into four parts. He mentioned that he wanted one organization that had four parts: a Bible Seminar, a Foreign Mission Board, a Home Mission Board, and an Administrative unit. He said that he would be in the center as the leader, and then he named others to the four posts: Bible Seminary—Heinrich Loewen; Foreign Missions—Willie Daikert; Home Missions—Bill Wagner; and Administration—Waldemar Reisch. His plan was for all of us to work together in all aspects of the plan. It worked, and once again I found myself as both a helper in getting a new school started and a professor as the head of the Department of Missions.

The school was both theologically strong and creative. Soon they moved out of the church into a large rented facility, and after two years they purchased a medium sized estate close to Bonn. This estate was just what the school needed to grow. The previous owner of the estate was the Green Party of Germany, who had used it as their national headquarters. They had a sign on the building that said, "From here we will change the World." We took over the motto. After a few more years the school had a four-year program and was teaching more Germans theology than any other institution in the country. Some of the students were taking theological education by distance. I continued to teach at the school until they hired three others to teach missions, and at that point I decided to remain an adjunct professor in name only.

Because I was a part of the school, we investigated the possibility of partnering with another school in the United States for accreditation, which we could not get in Germany. By that time, I had moved to California and was now teaching at Golden Gate Baptist Theological Seminary. We spoke at length about a partnership, and both schools were open to working together. In fact, Golden Gate contacted its accreditation agency, which said that the next step would be for a committee from the ATS to evaluate the school in Germany. They visited and gave the German seminary an A plus rating. The way was now clear for such a partnership. The plan was for Golden Gate to offer a master's degree in Bonn; students would need to attend one more year on top of the four now offered. All was in place. Soon thereafter the ATS met to discuss our request for approval. Unbeknown to me, the president of Golden Gate had also submitted a proposal to have another partnership recognized. This one was with Rick Warren and Saddle Back Church. At the meeting, the committee chairman told Golden Gate's president that their committee would recognize only one of the seminary's requests and he needed to choose which one. He chose Saddle Back since it fit more into the purpose of GGBTS. Bonn was left outside.

Once again, the Lord moved. Bonn had previously had good relations with Dr. Paige Patterson at Southwestern Seminary, and they soon adopted our plan; a partnership between Southwestern and Bonn became a reality. Patterson proved to be a great blessing to the folks in Bonn. They now have a master's program that is recognized in the U.S. The school in Bonn keeps working and has used several IMB missionaries in teaching positions, including my son Mark Wagner, who has been a big help to the school. With lime I pulled away from the school to do other duties. This was my second retirement. One of the great blessings experienced by the school was the great leadership of the school. After Victor Zierat resigned, the leadership fell to three men who formed a *Troika*, a three headed leadership group. The three were Dr. Heinrich Derksen, president of the school, Gerhard Schmidt, the academic dean, and Dr. Friedhelm Jung, dean of the masters' program. All three have remained in their position for many years, thus giving the school continuity. With time Dr. Derksen gained a great acceptance among religious and political leaders in German and other countries, thus giving the school a much higher profile in that country.

Haus Wittgenstein Home of the Bibelseminar Bonn

Joining the Faculty of Golden Gate Baptist Theological Seminary

By the mid-1990s I was still with the Foreign Mission Board of the Southern Baptists. I enjoyed the job, but in 1994 we were scheduled to go home on furlough. I had contact with Tom Wolf, who was the head of the mission's department at Golden Gate. He found out that I was available, and he asked me to spend a year as the missionary in residence. After this year, the school began to look for a professor to take the position of the Chair of Evangelism at the school. Because I was already there, I became a prime candidate. I was soon asked to take the position, but I was still a missionary. We looked at the rules for retirement from the Board and discovered that after serving a minimum of thirty years and reaching the age of 60, we could officially retire and become emeritus missionaries. We met the two requirements, so we took the option to retire and take the position offered by Golden Gate. We were now full time at our third seminary. This was my third retirement

Golden Gate Seminary helped us to purchase a house in the area, and I settled down to live out my life as a "Full Professor of Evangelism and Missions." The time in Golden Gate was very enjoyable. The other faculty members were all friendly, and the school was more mature than I was used to. I worked there for the next ten years, but when I reached the age of 70, I was told that there was an unwritten rule that professors would retire at that age. Since I was now active with other projects, retirement sounded good; thus, we went into retirement for the fourth time.

Becoming a Part of Olivet University

Up to this point the Lord had used me to help start two seminaries, but He was not yet done with me. There was another school that He wanted to start, and I was a part of its founding. This school is now known as Olivet University.

It all started as I was sitting in my office at Golden Gate when I was still teaching. The phone rang and on the other end there was a very soft-spoken young lady who said to me, "Dr. Wagner, Dr. Jang would like to know if you would be willing to come and work at Olivet University as the Academic Dean." My response was, "Who is Dr. Jang, what is Olivet University, and where is it located?" She then suggested that maybe I could come to San Francisco and meet with Dr. Jang. I agreed. In our meeting, Dr. Jang presented his plans for a full Christian university. It was to have six colleges, with Theology being the first. He wanted me to help. I asked if I could do this part time since I had a good position at Golden Gate, and he agreed. Later, I got the agreement from our own leadership at Golden Gate for the arrangement. I was now working as an academic dean in the basement of a large building in San Francisco, assigned to help create a university.

I later asked Dr. Jang how he ever came to invite me, of all persons, to be the dean. He said that he had five criteria and I fit all five points: (1) live in the San Francisco Area, (2) be firmly committed to evangelism and missions, (3) have the necessary academic documents, (4) be an Anglo-American, and (5) have white hair. He also said He had prayed, and the Lord has led him to me after studying others. He explained that most of their staff and students came from Asia, and he wanted someone who could represent the school and be distinguished from them. He also wanted someone who was elderly, since age is highly respected in the Asian culture and he wanted the future leadership of the school to be given to those who were now students. I was chosen and one of my duties was to train and prepare the future leadership of the school.

Outing in Wagner's backyard in California for new Students from Olivet University

We started the school and later moved up several stories in the same building. After two years, we moved to a nice facility with more room in downtown San Francisco. We began six colleges: Theology, Music, Art and Design, Journalism, Computer Technology, and Business.

Today all the colleges are functioning well. As one studies the list, it is apparent that all have something to do with using the Internet to win the world. Dr. Jang felt that through university students and the Internet, we can have the most success with making disciples of all nations. With time we added other professors, including Dr. Ray Tallman, a World Class Islamic Scholar, who was with me at Golden Gate, and Dr. Tom Cowley, a businessman in the area. A little later we were joined by Dr. Don Tinder, a former missionary to Belgium who had worked with me at the ETF. These men formed what was known as the senior faculty; we were often called "The Four Wise Men" by the students. Later, Dr. Merill Smoak was elected as one of the senior faculty. His specialty was music.

Over time I was asked to fill different positions, including Dean of the School of Theology, Academic Dean, International President, and finally President of the University. This was a position that I never thought I would have, but now the boy who barely made it through grade school was a university president. After I served in that position for three years, I retired for the fifth time and the school asked Dr. Tracy David, a young African American lady whom we had discipled, to replace me. My job was to prepare the younger generation to eventually take over the leadership of the school. Once again, this had been successful. The school gave me the title of "President Emeritus of Olivet University."

One of my jobs at Olivet was to become the founder and director of their doctoral program, which included both the Ph.D. and the Doctor of Ministry. I created the Ph.D. program on the same basis as what we had done with the ETF. Again, I looked for a highly qualified faculty and chose twelve top flight evangelical professors from six countries to be our Doctoral faculty. This worked well for the first four years, but when we applied for accreditation of the PhD. Degree, I was told that it had to fit better into the American system; thus, we changed it. In the first fifteen years of the existence of the University, the doctoral program, now named the Zinzendorf School of Doctoral Studies, granted 12 Ph.D. degrees and 93 Doctor of Ministry degrees. After a few years, the reins of the doctoral program were given over to Dr. Donald Tinder, and I was asked to form a new Institute for Global Strategic Studies. My next challenge was to create a think tank type of an institute to study how we best can win the world to Jesus Christ.

Doctoral Faculty for Olivet University

Chapter 14

Future Possibilities

> "You take all the experience and judgment of men
> over 50 out of the world and there would not be
> enough left to run it."
> – Henry Ford

Paul Harvey often closed his program with a short story with a poignant ending. He would introduce the ending by saying, "Now for the rest of the story." The ending was generally a surprise, but it would help to illustrate what he wanted his listeners to know. Now, after retiring five times, I am coming to the rest of the story. Once when I was a young preacher and was contemplating the life of Polycarp and his 85 years of service, I asked myself what I would do when I got over 80 years of age. My work was always with young people, but what could I do when I was old. I settled the question by saying "I would minister in a senior citizens home." There is always something to do for God.

I recently returned from preaching to over 60 professors of missions from Asia. On that continent old age is a sign of wisdom, and the Asians will shower a great amount of respect on those who are old. This is not true in the Western world. When I was getting ready to retire from Golden Gate Seminary, I overheard one student being thankful that now they would get some younger professors. When I went to Olivet, which was just across the Bay but where most of the students were Asians, they rejoiced that they had some older and wiser professors. Cultural differences are sometimes difficult to understand. As I approached the age of 80, I spent several days in prayer trying to decide what I could now do with my life. God reminded me that Moses was 80 when he had the burning bush experience, and for the next 40 years he was greatly used by God. Joshua was 84 when God told him to lead the Israelites into the promised land. Abraham lived to the ripe old age of 172 and remained active up to the end. I prayed that God would give me at least ten more years to serve Him in some capacity. I believe that he has honored my request. Several years ago, I approached Dr. Jang of Olivet University and asked him, "Now that I was now over 80, should I continue to work for Olivet? He informed me that the president of Olivet University in Korea was now 94, so not to worry.

Dreaming of Helping the SBC Be More Strategic

In the early part of this century I began to do more studying on strategy development. Why is it that some groups are having more success in growth than Southern Baptists? After all, we have the correct theology, great leadership, and wonderful institutions, but the Muslims, the Jehovah's Witnesses, and the Mormons are all growing at a faster rate than are Southern Baptists. There must be a reason, so I decided to do an in-depth study on the strategy of those groups plus that of the homosexual movement. I discovered that in each case they have a well-planned out strategy that is working. When I talked with some of our evangelical leaders about what others were doing, they just brushed it off by saying that these groups are either cults or false religions. I feel that we can still learn from them.

I studied the Mormon approach and was deeply impressed on how they are using university students while they are still in school to form the backbone of their program. In looking at what they are doing, I took several of these principles and developed a program that I called the Nehemiah Project. I then contacted Bob Record at the North American Mission Board and Jerry Rankin at the International Mission Board. Bob was concerned since they were just launching a new program of church planting professors called the Nehemiah Project. He asked me to change the name. I renamed it "The New Antioch." Both Dr. Rankin and Dr. Record allowed me to make a presentation of my plans to them and to some of their key leaders. The results were that the changes I was recommending were too radical and they did not feel they could be instituted together with what they were already doing. Both felt that I should go ahead and try to get my plans off the ground as a para-church activity. I rejected this since we needed a broader base from which to operate.

Running for an SBC Office

Some leaders suggested that maybe if I held one of the three top offices of the convention I would have a better platform from which to push my ideas, so I ran for the office of second vice-president at the convention in Dallas, Texas. I was told that the person who makes a nomination has a strong impact on the response, so I asked Dr. Cal Guy, Mission Professor at Southwestern Seminary to nominate me. After the first round I was leading, but the next day I had a runoff with a Hispanic pastor from Texas. I lost. Two years later I tried for the first vice-president, but again I lost. The next year I tried again for the second vice-president slot, and

Chapter 14: Future Possibilities

this time I won. I felt that now I could do something about my plans. I spoke with another man who had held this position earlier, and he said that he had no more influence because of his position. The position was just honorary. He was right. The only position that has any power is that of the president, so two years later I allowed myself to be nominated for the position of President of the SBC. One other man, Dr. Al Mohler of Southern Seminary, announced, but he dropped out due to an illness. Another pastor from Atlanta was also nominated, and for a while it seemed as if it would by a two-man race, but neither of us were the candidate who had been handpicked by the leadership of the convention. Soon four others joined the race, including Dr. Johnny Hunt. He won on the first ballot with a majority. This ended my attempts to be involved in SBC politics.

Bill Wagner Leading the Southern Baptist Convention as the Second Vice President

Down Times

So much good has happened to me that I tend to forget the down times. I already mentioned the burn out I experienced while still in Salzburg, but there were three times when I could have died. The first was in Albuquerque when I had appendicitis. The second happened after we had been in California for a long time. It was Thanksgiving and Sally had gone to visit her cousin, Dr. Lynn Drake, who is a very accomplished physician who is a professor at the Harvard school of medicine. Sally left on the weekend before the Thanksgiving holiday and I was to follow on Tuesday. On the days before I was to leave, I noticed that I was short of breath. When I ran, I had trouble breathing, but then I would rest and run again. Also, since I take my blood pressure every day, I noticed a spike up in the count. On the plane to see Sally and Lynn, I had a little pain in my chest. I was met at the airport by both ladies, and we started to drive to Lynn's home. In the car I said, "Lynn, I do not think it is anything to worry about, but I have been short of breath, my blood pressure is high, and I have a little pain in my chest." Lynn looked at me and said we were going to the emergency room. "Lynn," I cried, "I am not that sick." In her professional way she said, "Shut up; we are going to the hospital". I repeated that I was not sick. We arrive at the hospital where she got a wheelchair for me. I told her I was not going to use it. Once again, she told me to shut up. I reluctantly got into the wheelchair. In the hospital they did an MRI on me and discovered that I had three blood clots in my lungs. It was good that I was in the hospital. I still did not feel bad, so Lynn and Sally decided to go home. They were going to move me to a hospital bed, but before they could move me, I had a terrible pain in my chest and could hardly breath. They called Sally and Lynn back, and I remember as I was about to lose conscienceless the doctor saying to me, "Stay with us, stay with us." I was almost gone. After one week in intensive care and another week in another ward, I was dismissed from the hospital. Had I not taken Lynn's advice that caused me to be in the emergency room when it hit, I would have died. Dr. Lynn and God took care of me.

A third time when I had a problem with my health took place in my hometown of Petaluma, Sally and I had been to a Bible Study. Before we went to bed Sally said she had a little pain in her chest, and I told her that if it got worse, we would take her to the hospital. In the middle of the night I got a real pain in my chest, so Sally took me to the hospital. In the emergency room they discovered that I had pancreatitis. I again spent a few days in intensive care. At that time, the doctors gave me several medicines to help. After about a week, they let me go home and I felt fine but two days later, I woke up and could barely move. I could not go from the bed to the chair. My muscles, which did not hurt, did not function. Again, they took me to the hospital, and they could not find out the problem. One doctor said I had pneumonia, and another said it was congestive heart failure. My lungs would not function, and they had to give me emergency oxygen to keep me alive. After two days one doctor discovered that I had taken the medicine Amiodarone. It is a harsh drug that can have some bad side effects. I was having a bad reaction to it. Medical books say that about 5 percent of those who take this medicine have a bad reaction and 2 percent die. I was at about 2.1 percent. Again, I almost died, but once again God was not through with me. I also had the prayers from thousands of people from many countries of the world. I was told that this medicine, unlike others, stays in the body for about six months. For that period, I had difficulty speaking, moving, and breathing, but after the six months I was again as good as new.

Despite three different episodes of almost dying, I knew that God had saved me for his service. My goal now is to break the record for the 100-meter dash for those 100 years or older. Currently, I am on track to do it.

Writing Books

Reading books was not one of my favorite pastimes, but strangely, writing books gives me great joy. I try to collect as much information on a given subject as possible and keep little cards handy so that I could write it down. Now in my office I have four large boxes of cards that contain sermon illustrations, quotes, and/or sermon outlines. Much of my information has been gained by visual learning or by scanning literature. Up to the time I began at Olivet, I had written three books, two of which were my dissertations for my doctoral degrees. At that point I wanted to help Evangelicals begin to think outside the box as far as strategic planning is concerned. I already mentioned several groups that I wanted to study, so I took these groups, added two more, and I began to write a book on how seven groups (I used the term groups because all were not religions or denominations) are planning for growth: the Southern Baptists (Evangelicals); the Assemblies of God (Charismatics); the Jehovah's Witnesses; the Mormons; the Muslims; the Homosexuals, and the three main cover organizations: The World Council of Churches, The Lausanne Movement, and the World Evangelical Alliance.

Each of these seven are growing, and I wanted to know why. Since I had much material on the Muslims from my time in the Middle East, I felt that I should start with them. The more I studied and the more I wrote, the more I realized that the material I had was far more than just a chapter but should become a complete book; thus my first more popular book, *How Islam Plans to Change the World*, came into being. It appeared at a time when many in the Western world were deeply concerned about the growth of Islam. The book seemed to hit the right chord, and it has sold over 10,000 copies. It has also been translated into German, Spanish, and Korean. Because of the success of the book, I have been invited to appear on more than forty television and radio stations to talk about the growth of Islam.

Working with the WEA

From the beginning of Olivet University, they have tried to support the work of the World Evangelical Alliance. Because of my interest with worldwide missions and with Olivet, it was natural that I too became interested in working with the WEA. Much of my contact was with Dr. Thomas Schirrmacher and the Theological Commission since my interest flowed through a theological university. I was able to attend many of their conferences and even lead in several large meetings of the leadership. My theme was always trying to help this important worldwide evangelical movement form a more compete strategy to win the world.

At one point I asked Dr. Schirrmacher how I could help. He suggested that I write a short book to present my ideas of strategy development. I decided to write this book together with my son Dr. Mark Wagner. *Can Evangelicals Really Change the World?* was published as one of the books in the WEA World of Theology Series. It studies the strategy of seven divergent denominations and groups. One African leader who read the book remarked that he had read many books that had 300 pages and he felt the authors could have said what needed to be said in 50 pages, but he wanted my book to say more and that it should have been longer than its100 pages. I kept it short because I wanted World Christian leaders to read it and I was told that busy people do not read long books.

Finding New Ways to Make a Difference

After retiring from the position of director of the doctoral program, I was asked to create a new Institute that was dedicated to strategic studies. We have now started the Olivet Institute for Global Strategic Studies. The purpose of this Institute is to find ways to help the worldwide Christian church to be more successful in winning the world to Christ. As I studied the various groups that were growing in the world, I discovered several keys to help us.

The first came from an Islamic source. Muslim Strategist Khervam Mural claims that Islam works at three levels: The Micro level, the level of individual persons and small organizations; the Meta level, the level of large groups, institutions, and structures; and the Mega level, the level of overall *ummah* and Muslim societies and states.

In applying these three levels to the six mentioned groups, I was surprised to discover that only three of the seven have a major strategy at the Mega level. They are the Mormons, the Muslims, and the Homosexuals. Sadly, Evangelicals and the Charismatics have concentrated solely on the first two levels. True, they have been successful at these levels, but there is a need to go up one level to the Mega. We can learn from the three that do operate on the Mega level.

Another important key that I discovered was what some evangelicals were calling the Seven Mountains of Culture, areas of life that need to be influenced for one to make an impact. The idea is that these are building blocks for every culture and that a strategy needs to be developed for each mountain. The original seven were Art and Theater; Business; Education; Religion; Family, Media; and Government. To these seven I added three more: Sports; Technology; and Military.

At the present time our Institute is gathering many who are working on dissertations and projects to help us in developing strategies for world evangelism. Since we are just in the beginning stages, it is difficult to know how much success we will enjoy in the future.

Keeping Fit

As mentioned earlier, I have always been interested in various sports and did compete in track in both high school and the university. From my student days on, I kept a record of how many miles or kilometers I run each day. At first, I thought it was a useless endeavor but later I have discovered that it is helpful to know how far I have run in my life.

For most of my adult life I have kept records of the distance I have run up to date as well as other health activities such as where I have run, my time running, my blood pressure, and my oxygen level. I found that this has helped to encourage me to keep fit. Several yeas ago I was written up in Runner's World Magazine for having run a minimum of 5 kilometers in over 1200 cities and towns in over 80 countries in the world. At the present time I have run over 100,000 kilometers which is over two times the circumference of the earth. Today I average over 3 kilometers a day. During my earlier days I ran 18 Marathons in over 10 countries.

Running the Flying Pig Marathon in Cincinnati

Not only do I run, but on an average of five days a week I play one to two hours of racquetball and work out with weights. I have been blessed with a strong body and while playing football I never received an injury to my body except for the concussions.

Another benefit from running, is that I can see many sights in the countries where I run. I have run around twenty-five state capitals in the U.S., around the wall of Jerusalem, around the Sea of Galilee, around the Colosseum in Rome, around the Kremlin in Moscow, on the Great Wall of China, etc. I have seen far more than most tourists by just running in cities where I have visited. While being a consultant, my area extended from the deserts of the Middle East to the icefields of Siberia in Russia. Thus, I have also run in many various climates. For instance, the hottest place I have run in was in Saudi Arabia where it was 129 degrees Fahrenheit and the coldest was in Siberia when it was 28 degrees below zero Fahrenheit.

Chapter 14: Future Possibilities

Also, during my many runs I have had some interesting experiences. In Lower Egypt, while wearing my red running suit, I was stoned for being the devil, and in Marseille, France I stopped a mugging. Two men were ready to jump a prosperous looking older man when they saw me across the street. They stopped when they saw me and did nothing if I could see them. I stayed there until the man got away.

One day, I was staying in the Jewish part of Jerusalem with some of our missionaries and I decided to run. I was warned to stay on the Jewish side and not to go on the Arab side. I started to run and without knowing where I was, I came upon a group of young Palestinian men who were playing soccer. I then realized I was in the wrong part of the city. Whey they saw me one of them yelled at me and then they all began to run towards me some throwing rocks. I remembered that the Arabs love the Austrians since both Hitler and Eichmann were Austrians. As they came towards me, I cried our "Nemsa, Nemsa" which is the Arabic word for Austria. One who spoke English asked me if I came from Austria. I said yes and they then invited me to play soccer with them which I did. They were then genuinely nice to me.

On another occasion, I was traveling from South Africa to Namibia for a MasterLife Workshop and the missionary stopped at a small Inn somewhere along the road for our nights rest. It was in the middle of a large barren area. Without thinking where I was, I got up early in the morning and began to run. I came down the road into a small valley and heard a loud terrifying cry. I looked up and I had a pack of hyenas all around me. I thought, "Are hyenas dangerous? Without any more thinking I got out of there as fast as I could. Later I was told they can be extremely dangerous in a pack as they were. I have genuinely enjoyed my various running experiences.

Once my desire to run in many different countries just about got me not trouble. I was traveling in Malawi in Africa. We were going from the capital city to the second largest city where our mission was located. As we were travelling on the road the missionary pointed off to the right and said that just fifty meters away was Mozambique. The road was just in Malawi territory. I had my running gear with me and asked if we could stop for a half hour so that I could run in a new country. He agreed and we stopped, and I changed my clothes. I got ready to run when one of the Africans with us mentioned that I needed to look out for the landmines. I was told they had put many there to discourage people going over the border. I did not run in Mozambique.

While I was a student at the university, I read in Luke 2:32 that Jesus "grew in wisdom and stature, and in favor with God and man." I was taught that Jesus was concerned about four different areas of life which were academic (wisdom), physical (stature), spiritual (favor with God), and social (favor with man). During my life I have tried to keep these four aspects of like in balance. Approximately every four months I make an evaluation of my life and rate myself in all four areas. Often, I will see that I have neglected one area thus I need to be sure that I am growing in all four areas.

Being Active at the Micro level

General Boykin, a highly decorated general of the U.S. military, gave me some insights that have helped me. He stated that every military in the world divides its leadership into three levels: the Tactical Level, which is those who are fighting on the battlefield; the Operational Level, those who are behind the lines doing the planning; and the Strategic Level, those who are in Washington doing the strategy planning.

He mentioned to me that a mistake often made by leaders is that they attempt to operate at two or three levels at the same time, and if they do, they lose focus and become ineffective. Many times, I have thought about this. Much of my strategy for life has been multi-tasking; thus, I have tried to do work at different levels with the results having an effect at the different levels. I continue to see if this can be effective. Currently, I am now the pastor of an Iranian church in my community, which leads me to work at the Micro level, I continue to teach at Olivet which is Macro work, while still working at the Mega level with the Institute. General Boykins was right it is difficult to work on two or three different levels at the same time, but I still see that a worker for God must have a personal contact with individuals in order to not lose the perspective that it is individual persons who need to know Jesus. I continue to work on all three levels at the same time, but I cannot recommend it to others.

How Do You Measure Success?

If in grade school they had given an award for the "most unlikely to succeed," I would have won it hands down. The same could be true for my time in junior high, but God had a different plan for my life. With the help of family, football, friends, and faith, God has been able to do extraordinary things with the ordinary man I am. At the fiftieth anniversary of my high school graduating class, one of my co-students came by and said that he thought I had been the most successful of the class. I am not sure about this; however, in my life I have been able to accomplish what I would never have thought possible as a child.

Here are some of my accomplishments:

1. Earn one bachelor's degree and one master's degree
2. Become a licensed engineer in the State of New Mexico
3. Run a medium sized engineering business
4. Earn two doctors' degrees
5. Play division I football and run track in university
6. Start 10 churches in 4 countries
7. Serve overseas for 31 years as a missionary
8. Visit over 100 countries
9. Lecture in seminaries in 35 countries
10. Help disciple 24,000 through MasterLife Discipleship Training
11. See over 200 young people come to faith at the Youth Center
12. Encourage 4 young people who are now ministers in Europe
13. Ordain 22 young men into the ministry
14. Help start a Bible School and three seminaries
15. Help found a university
16. Create two Doctoral programs
17. Mentor 8 PhD. students and 15 D. Miss Students
18. Serve as president of Olivet University
19. Serve as Chairman of the Board for the Christian Post for five years
20. Run at least 5 kilometers in over 1200 cities and towns in the world
21. Run 18 marathons in ten countries
22. Author 5 books and many magazine articles
23. Serve as Second Vice-President of the Southern Baptist Convention

To top all of this off, possibly my greatest achievement is the wonderful family that God gave me. I have a great wife, Sally, and two exceptionally talented children, Candice, and Mark. Mark and Carrie have two daughters, Kate and Natalie, and Candice and Scott have Sophia and Matthew. All in the family have a deep belief in Jesus Christ. Another blessing is that all four of the grandchildren are either finished with their college education or will be soon. Sally and I have lived to see God's continued blessings on our extended family flow into the lives of our grandchildren.

Conclusion

Jim McKinnon, and his lovely wife Marie, are close friend of ours going all the way back to the Hermosa Drive days. Jim was at one time one of the top life insurance salesmen in the country. His home base was in the economically poor region of New Mexico; thus, his success was even more remarkable. As I talked with him about what he had accomplished, he gave me several tips that have helped me in my ministry. One has to do with the type of people that one is most likely to influence. He stated, "The age group that you will be able to influence the most will be those who are between ten years younger or ten years older than yourself." I have found this to be true. When I was young, I was great in working with preteens at the church. Later this emphasis changed as I worked with university students, then pastors, then church leaders, and now with retired people. One of my discoveries in the way God works is that He is ready to use all our talents for his work. He will develop other skills that compensate for our weaknesses if necessary. When we think we are too old to be used by God, He will give us a ministry that will reach those in our age group. God is never through with us no matter what our age or our skills. For 62 years I have served Him, and He has done me no wrong. How great is our God?

When I was a young person, even though I enjoyed running, there was one area of scripture that did not mean much to me, but today I begin to understand what Paul was describing. This scripture is II Timothy 4:7-8. Paul wrote "I have fought the good fight, I have finished the race, I have kept the Faith. I know there is in store for me the crown of righteousness, which the Lord, the righteous judge, will award to me on that day – and not only to me, but also to all who have longed for his appearance." As I get older, I can better understand Paul's feelings about life and purpose. I too look forward to the time when I shall receive my crown of righteousness and will live with Jesus for all eternity.

Before Jesus Christ ascended into heaven, He gathered his disciples and gave them the command to "Go and make disciples of all Nations, teaching them to observe all things I have taught you, and lo, I am with you even until the end of the age." I do not think that his command has been changed: every Chisinau still must live his or her whole life in a way to help the world know that Jesus Christ is Lord. It is my hope that this book can help others to become more involved in carrying out the Great Commission. Amen.

www.ingramcontent.com/pod-product-compliance
Lightning Source LLC
Chambersburg PA
CBHW070918160426
43193CB00011B/1515